PRAISE FOR
WHAT IF...WHY NOT?

"Wow, talk about feeling seen and understood! The book offers practical advice and a clear roadmap for building a solid foundation after college, guiding you through the unspoken. It's a powerful reminder that no matter where you start, your journey is full of limitless potential and purpose."

Gisel Ureña, Schneider Electric, Leadership Development Program, AI Product Owner

.

"*What If...Why Not?* provides essential guidance for first-gen students searching for their first job out of college. What sets it apart from other guidebooks is its emphasis on the softer skills that ensure that first-gen jobseekers both survive the job search and thrive in their new roles. Whether dealing with Imposter Syndrome, incorporating self-care, or creating a personalized Board of Directors, "*What If...Why Not?*" takes a holistic and comprehensive approach to a stressful, nerve-racking process."

Kelly Glew, President, The Steppingstone Foundation

"I could not be more delighted than to give my full endorsement to this very timely and excellent guidebook for first-generation students. As one of them, I wish I had this invaluable advice available to me in such a concise manner when I was finishing my undergraduate career.

The guidebook is put together under the fine hand of Susan Gershenfeld, a first-class professional with whom I had the pleasure to work with when we created the Illinois Promise Program. I credit her, and the team she chose, for the spectacular success of that program.

In this guidebook she has built on her experiences to provide eminently readable advice to students as they consider entering professional life. Just how does one make that transition? Students outside of schools like engineering and business rarely encounter these ideas and even then there is a special case to be made for first-gen students as the guidebook so clearly points out.

In full recognition of the fact that the guidebook is written for students, I believe it should be used by faculty/staff as they prepare their students."

Richard Herman, Former Chancellor,
University of Illinois, Urbana-Champaign

"What If...Why Not? is an exceptionally useful and well-written guide for first-generation college graduates transitioning into their careers. The processes outlined in the book are relevant to all graduates and insights are supported by research and real world experience. Reading this book will take the anxiety and confusion out of the college-to-career transition."

Pat Canavan, CEO Waymark Analytics and Senior Vice President, Global Governance, Motorola Inc. (retired)

"Finally, a comprehensive guide encompassing all the information a first generation or any college graduate would need to fully navigate the treacherous waters landing their first employment opportunity and beyond. "

Dennis L. Dabney, Former Senior Vice President in Human Resources, Kaiser Permanente Health Plan & Hospitals

"With over 20 years of experience in student career counseling, I can attest to the value of *What If...Why Not?* for all college students about to graduate, but especially for first-generation college students as they prepare to enter the job market. The guidebook is practical, accessible, and should be a go-to resource for this generation of college graduates."

Pnina Steiner, Business Career Services Director (Retired), University of Illinois, Urbana-Champaign

"What a fantastic college-to-career guide and roadmap! In this book, Susan provides accessible and actionable advice to bridge the gap between college learning and workplace success. She has completely demystified the unspoken rules of professional culture, career advancement, and personal success that many first-gen students are never taught. If you're a first-gen student about to enter the workforce—or someone who supports them — *What if…Why Not?* is a must-read! You will feel prepared, not overwhelmed. I will be recommending this book to all first-gen students we serve."

Monica Kachru,
Founder and Board Chair, Anaya Scholars

A **Guidebook** for First-Generation Students
Transitioning from College to Career

WHAT IF...
WHY NOT?

SUSAN GERSHENFELD

WITH CONTRIBUTIONS FROM LOIS BENISHEK,
SHANICKA S. BURDINE, ANNALEA FORREST & JANEL MCNUCKLE

Editing, design, distribution by Bublish

ISBN: 978-1-647049-84-3 (eBook)
ISBN: 978-1-647049-85-0 (paperback)

To first-generation college graduates -
you are living proof that dreams are not limited by
circumstances.

ACKNOWLEDGMENTS

The trust first-generation college graduates have placed in me to share their advice and stories—so that others from similar circumstances can benefit—is a gift I will always cherish.

I am deeply appreciative of my former college students and colleagues who took the time to review drafts of this manuscript and offer valuable feedback, including Alexandra, Baozhen, Gisel, Grace, Khanh, Lois, Pnina, and Richard. Your insights made this book stronger.

A heartfelt thank you to my contributors—Annalea, Janel, Lois, and Shanicka—for generously sharing your expertise. A special shout-out to Lois, whose editorial skills were truly instrumental in refining this guidebook. Thanks to her keen eye, the content flows more smoothly, and her steady sense of humor made the process enjoyable.

Finally, I am endlessly grateful for my husband, Joel, whose unwavering support and enthusiasm made this endeavor even more meaningful.

CONTENTS

INTRODUCTION

Hey there! If you're reading this, you're probably in a pretty exciting (and maybe nerve-racking) phase of life: transitioning from college to your first job. As a soon-to-be first-generation college grad, you've already proven you've got the grit, smarts, and determination to break barriers and reach big goals. But let's face it—this next step can feel like uncharted territory.

That's where this guidebook comes in. Think of it as a quick, friendly road map designed just for you. *What If... Why Not?* symbolizes an empowering mindset. It encourages us to continue dreaming big (what if?) and taking action without fear or self-doubt (why not?). It represents an invitation to explore opportunities beyond what we might initially think is possible and to challenge assumptions about our potential.

Each chapter is organized based on advice from fellow first-gen graduates who've been where you are. How did we get their advice? About one hundred completed a survey, then about twenty-five voluntarily participated in focus groups, and about a dozen first-gen college graduates shared their stories through interviews and other means.

And four first-gen college graduates contributed by writing portions of this guidebook. As a mental health professional, Annalea wrote the chapter on addressing common personal barriers and, together with Lois (a consulting psychologist), identified key strategies and tools to help address these common personal barriers. Janel and Shanicka, human resource professionals, added tips that you'll see throughout the guidebook. As the lead author, I, too, am a first-generation college graduate. I have had the privilege and honor of working with first-generation college students over the past fifteen years, with the last five years focusing exclusively on supporting people like you on college-to-career transitions.

We've kept it short enough to read in about an hour or two but loaded it with actionable tips on everything from landing your first professional position to growing your career, working with mentors, managing money, and balancing work with other things that are important in your life. You'll find resources at the end of the book for more in-depth information—links to podcasts, videos, assessments, and additional key readings. So read it from start to finish or peruse chapters that meet your immediate needs.

Ready to dive in and tackle this next chapter? Let's do it together!

CHAPTER 1

BEFORE THE JOB SEARCH

I wish I knew how to do interviews and job search better. I think it is back to that less-privileged background that I had with the mindset to find a job as fast as I could and to focus on just having a job, any reasonable job, rather than taking a little bit more time and effort to find a job that can grow my career better, which is something that someone with a better safety net can afford to do.

—Khanh Ngo

When you think about searching for your first post-college job, what do you think about? Are you like Khanh, where you focus on having any reasonable job even if you might later regret the choice? First jobs matter, especially for women and employees not in the tech sector. Research shows that if you are underemployed in your first position post-college (that is, the position you fill does not require a college degree), you are significantly more likely to be underemployed ten years out[i]. Let me repeat: first jobs matter.

I have spent the past fifteen years supporting low-income and mostly first-gen students (that is, students whose parents did not graduate from a four-year college) through college and in their transition to work. The focus of most universities is on supporting students through to graduation. What I witnessed, as a result, was a pattern where students were so oriented around getting good grades in the march to graduation that they weren't building professional connections, and they weren't prioritizing hands-on experiences and internships. I was less worried for the students who were in majors that led to well-defined careers, such as engineering, nursing, and business. But students in the humanities, in some social sciences, and even in some sciences were at a loss for what to do after completing their degrees. It was heartbreaking to see hardworking students earn a degree and then be underemployed. Do you know how intensive the coursework involved with earning a degree in animal science is? Imagine how you'd feel if you ended up working in retail at Petco after graduation, which is exactly what happened to a first-gen student who excelled in science but was not ready for what happened afterward.

That's when I shifted my focus to support first-gen students transitioning from college to career. Why? So much of students' efforts were placed on earning the degree and much less so on what followed. They were playing by the spoken rules (get good grades, earn the degree, and apply to posted positions). They weren't paying attention to the unspoken rules (build connections and transferable skills). And, unfortunately, the services offered through many university career centers are underutilized by first-gen, low-income students, probably for the reasons cited above—a focus on what is immediately in front of them.

Thinking back, I, too, fit into that category as a first-gen student, primarily focusing on the spoken rules.

There's prep work needed before you begin searching for your first professional position after college. This chapter focuses on this prep work—knowing yourself and being prepared to market yourself.

Know Yourself

I remember graduating from college and one of my classmates said she wasn't sure what type of work she wanted to do, but she knew what she didn't want to do. At the time I thought, *That's great, she's narrowing down her choices.* I still think that way.

If you aren't sure what you want to do, here are some ways to help you figure it out.

1. **Assessing Interests and Abilities.** What activities do you find engaging and energizing? If you don't know, record your activities at least twice a week over a two-week period. These activities could include researching a topic, preparing a

SUSAN GERSHENFELD

presentation, leading a small group discussion,
analyzing data, planning an event, and so on.
On a scale of 1–10 (1 = low and 10 = high), how
would you rate these activities based on how engaged you are with the activity, and on a similar
scale, how would you rate your energy level?
After recording and assessing your activities,
what patterns do you see emerging? What skills
are required for the activities in which you are
highly engaged and energized? What did you
learn about yourself? For instance, do you prefer
solitary work, public-facing work, creative work,
or routine work? This is particularly important as
a first-gen student since you may not have people who know you *and* who know about career
opportunities that would be a good fit for you.

Assessing Interests and Activities

Logging Activities

	Engagement	Energy
_____	lo ||| hi	lo ||| hi
_____	lo ||| hi	lo ||| hi
_____	lo ||| hi	lo ||| hi
_____	lo ||| hi	lo ||| hi

2. **Career Assessments.** Even as you're approaching or in your last year of college, you might need to take or retake a career assessment to learn more about how well a variety of careers could suit you. There are different types of assessments focusing on specific areas, such as skills, interests, or values. Check out assessments that are offered through your university's career center, state and government tools, and popular assessment tools that are at no cost or a nominal fee. (See Resources at the end of the guidebook for website links.) Whichever assessments you take, ask yourself questions such as: What did I learn that resonates with me, and why does it resonate? What did I learn that doesn't seem to fit me and why? How am I going to utilize this information going forward? You may know about popular careers, such as those portrayed on TV and in movies, but there are dozens of careers that you have likely never heard about but that might be a great fit for you. Career placement professionals can also be helpful here.

3. **Informational Interviews.** Conducting informational interviews is an excellent way to learn about a potential career field by interviewing someone over the phone, virtually, or in person. People like to talk about themselves and their careers, especially to college students who are exploring their own career options. It's also a

great source for networking during your job search (discussed in chapter 2 as "informational meetings"). How do you find a person to interview? Your existing network, university career services, and LinkedIn are all possibilities. How long should the informational interview take? You should ask for twenty to thirty minutes. In addition to asking questions, do some homework in advance so you are not coming to the conversation uninformed. Learn about the industry, the organization, the department, the position, and the person you will be interviewing. You'll also need to prepare an elevator pitch (more on that later). After completing each informational interview, reflect on what you've learned. (See informational interview template below.)

Informational Interview Meetings:

What I Learned & Next Steps

Name/Title/Organization:_____

Phone Number/Email:_____

Date of Interview:_____

What sounds appealing about the type of work they are doing / have done and why?

_____

_____

What skills do I have that might be used in this type of work?

_____

_____

What skills would I need to develop to do this type of work?

_____

_____

What doesn't sound appealing about the type of work they are doing / have done and why?

_____

_____

Based on this discussion, how enthusiastic am I about this type of work and why?

_____

_____

Not at all   Moderately   Extremely

0   1   2   3   4   5   6   7   8   9   10

Based on this discussion, what other types of jobs/careers would I like to look into?

_____

_____

People This Person Suggested I Also Speak With:

_____

Name:_____

Organization:_____

Contact Information:_____

How will I be introduced to them?_____

_____

Questions to Ask Others During Future Informational Interviews:_____

_____

Skills Identification

If you're not sure what skills you have to offer because of a lack of a relevant internship, think about skills you've acquired elsewhere. Perhaps there are skills you've gained through class assignments, student clubs, volunteer experiences, high school or work study jobs, or just in general through life. These are called transferable skills, which employers value and seek out in potential employees. Alongside your educational achievements, these skills can demonstrate readiness to contribute meaningfully to an organization, even without extensive work experience. For example:

- **Communication skills.** Whether it's speaking, writing, or nonverbal communication, being able to clearly express yourself and collaborate with others is essential for any role.

- **Problem-solving / critical thinking skills.** These skills help you tackle challenges, make informed decisions, and adapt to change. They also show you can bring fresh ideas and solutions to an organization.

- **People skills (emotional intelligence).** Emotional intelligence is about understanding and managing your own emotions while being able to connect with and influence others. It's essential for teamwork, building strong relationships, accepting constructive feedback from peers and supervisors, and creating a positive work environment.

- **Time management skills.** Being able to prioritize tasks and meet deadlines are both crucial for staying productive and ensuring things run smoothly in any job.

If you're having difficulty identifying transferable skills beyond these four examples, consider thinking about interesting personal stories from your life. With each story, what was your goal? What did you accomplish? What were some hurdles or obstacles, and how did you overcome them? What was the outcome? What people skills were involved (e.g., motivating and negotiating)? What skills were used with data or ideas (e.g., planning, organizing, and working with numbers)? What skills did you use with things (e.g., assembling and operating)? Are any of these skills transferrable?

Personal character traits also matter. For example, do you demonstrate good judgment? Do you hustle to meet deadlines? Are you well organized? Do you work independently but also know when to ask for help? Do you hold up well under pressure? How would you assess yourself in relation to these traits? These are some character traits that are highly desirable by hiring managers. What other character traits are you proud of that will benefit your future workplace? As a first-gen student, you may not think these personal characteristics matter as much as tangible skills, but employers know that these are just as important when it comes to finding a successful new employee.

Market Yourself

Unless you have had an internship where your employer knows how you can contribute to the organization's success or someone you know offers you a role, you'll need to market yourself to find your first position after college. The job isn't going to find you. It is worth reading that sentence again! Marketing yourself includes writing a résumé and cover letter, creating a LinkedIn profile, and perfecting an elevator pitch. Some soon-to-be college graduates with a portfolio should consider setting up a website, or for social media creatives, consider setting up a free bio landing page on Linktree. The first four most common marketing tools are briefly covered below.

1. Résumé

Before it lands in the hands of a recruiter who will take about ten seconds reviewing it, your résumé must get past AI systems and automated readers. It is also worth reading that sentence again! To get your résumé past the AI systems and automated readers, match the language in the job description. Tailor your résumé specifically to the role and organization you're applying for. For example, if the job calls for experience with R, Python, or other statistical programming tools, be sure to include R, Python, or whatever software you've worked with. It's all about showing them you have exactly what they're looking for!

There are numerous résumé examples online that you can check out. Below are some key tips for writing your résumé followed by examples:

- **Recent college grads should keep it to one page.** A résumé is a marketing document designed to get you an interview, not a biography. Highlight the most relevant and impactful experiences tailored to the job for which you're applying. Your bullets points should indicate your accomplishments and results associated with that task.

- **Make it readable.** This means using white space (leave space for at least 1" margins, double space between subheadings, use 12 pt. font). Prioritize white space over cramming too much on a page. Fonts like Arial and Calibri are easy on the eyes.

- **Include your GPA if it's 3.5 or higher.** Employers, particularly in competitive industries like finance, consulting, engineering, and in certain entry roles, often view a high GPA as a sign of a strong work ethic and academic performance. Alternatively, if your GPA associated with the major courses (e.g., psychology, accounting) is significantly higher than your overall GPA, then simply mention your major GPA.

Education

[Your University Name] — *Bachelor of Arts in Sociology Graduated: May 2024 | GPA: 3.6/4.0*

Relevant Coursework: Social Research Methods, Statistics, Public Policy Analysis, Writing for the Social Sciences

---

- **Include a summary sentence.** This makes it easier for people to understand right away what you're looking for and how you can add value. Use this sentence as an opportunity to showcase a skill or characteristic that may not be displayed elsewhere in your résumé.

Professional Summary

Motivated and adaptable recent college graduate with a bachelor's degree in [Your Major], seeking to apply strong communication, leadership, and problem-solving skills in a dynamic, mission-driven organization. First-generation college graduate with a proven track record of perseverance, initiative, and community engagement.

- **Use the CAR (Challenge-Action-Result) method for bullet points.** What Challenge did you face, what Actions did you take to address it, and what was the positive quantifiable Result or impact of your efforts? This format makes achievements and contributions more compelling to potential employers.

Accomplishments

Student Assistant—*Office of Student Success, [University]
Aug 2022–May 2023*

- Addressed students' lack of awareness of campus resources by developing weekly outreach emails and organizing info tables at events, leading to a 40 percent increase in inquiries about tutoring services.

- **Proofread, then have someone else proofread.** After proofreading, read your résumé backward to triple-check there are no errors. One error can be interpreted as not paying attention to detail and automatically remove you from consideration.

HR Pro Tip:

Utilize AI services such as Grammarly and ChatGPT to review your résumé (and cover letter) for grammatical and spelling errors.

In addition to a formal résumé, I like to create a résumé addendum. I once saw an example when I interned over the summer in a hospital human resources department. The woman who sent a résumé addendum was flown in from another state to be interviewed. Since then, every time I have applied for a position, I've used the same technique and have been invited for an interview. Crafting a résumé addendum for each position in which you apply illustrates that you are analytical, organized, and qualified to a hiring manager, and it helps you begin preparing for the upcoming interview. I'll briefly explain it here, and an example follows.

A résumé addendum is submitted along with your résumé. It is also one page. It has your name and contact information on the top. The content is in a two-column format. In the left column, include in bullet format the requirements from the job description with a heading "(Job Title) Requirements." In the right column, include in bullet format your knowledge, skills, and experience as it relates to each of the job requirements, quantifying to the fullest extent possible. Use the header for the right column "My Relevant Knowledge, Skills & Experience." The spacing should line up in both columns, so whatever the first requirement is in the left column, it's easy to see the relevant knowledge, skills, and experience in the right column and so on with each requirement and personal entry that follows. An abbreviated example is on the next page. The CAR method and proofreading approach used for your résumé applies to this document, too.

Can you appreciate how creating this document would help a hiring manager do their job and help you prepare for the interview?

Resume Addendum Example
Jane Smith
Janesmith@gmail.com
Public Relations Officer (Job #1000)

Requirements for Public Relations Officer Position	My Relevant Knowledge, Skills & Experience
• Bachelor's degree in Public Relations or a related field	• BA Communications, English minor. ASU, 2024. Cum laude.
• Excellent verbal and written communication skills	• Wrote 25 press releases during summer internship, resulting in news coverage in five major outlets.
• Strong organizational skills and attention to detail	• Planned 3 major events attracting over 250 attendees each. Secured sponsorships totaling $10,000.
• Ability to multitask and manage deadlines in a fast-paced environment	• Worked part-time throughout all four years of college.
• Proficiency with social media	• Proficient in Cision and Meltwater

2. Cover Letter

Always submit a customized cover letter along with your résumé, unless the application instructions explicitly ask you not to. Why? Because a cover letter is an opportunity to communicate that you have done some preliminary research on the organization and have a genuine (and enthusiastic) interest in applying. It also offers another chance to highlight a potential fit between your qualifications and the position requirements.

The best cover letter I've read conveyed in the first sentence that the applicant understood the organization and role, and why she was applying. It was engaging to read. It didn't start with, "Please accept my application for the position of [XX]." She *concisely* explained how her background and skill set could add value in furthering the organization's goals. That was all communicated in one page; no one is going to read a longer cover letter.

While you can also read a variety of cover letter examples online, here are the mechanics for writing a personalized cover letter for each position in which you are applying.

First Paragraph—*Introduction*. Your introductory paragraphs should be no longer than three or four sentences. As noted above, state what you understand about the organization and role, and why you are interested in applying for the position (name the position title).

Paragraph two (and maybe three)—*Body.* These paragraphs should highlight the strongest aspects of your résumé in relation to the job description. When writing this section, keep in mind that the reader is wondering why they should hire you, so convince them in your own words. Do not repeat wording from your résumé—add something new or provide insight into your résumé accomplishments. You can do this in bullet points. If you are including a résumé addendum, you can point to this document in this section as well. For example: "For further information, please refer to my attached résumé addendum, which matches the position requirements with my knowledge, skills, and experience."

Final Paragraph—*Closing.* Include something about the organization that makes it of interest to you. Perhaps it's their products that you use regularly or the values they embody as an organization. Thank the person for taking the time to review your résumé and consider your candidacy for the position.

As with the résumé, human eyes will only take a few seconds to review your cover letter. As such, make it readable (include white space, 12 pt. font, Arial or Calibri) and error-free by proofreading it, having someone else proofread it, then reading it backward.

Here are some other details to help you:

- The cover letter and résumé should match formatting (font type, margins, etc.).

- Add date, address (no zip code needed if submitting electronically).

- Include job title and job code (if available) before the salutation.

- Personalize the cover letter with a name (if possible) or by title in the salutation (e.g., "Dear Ms. Jones" or "Dear Recruiter," not "Dear Sir/Madam," not "To Whom it May Concern").

- Submit cover letter, résumé, and résumé addendum in one file if sent electronically. Name the file something that is convenient to the organization (e.g., Last Name_Job Code or Last Name_Position Title).

3. LinkedIn Profile

Did you know that having a great LinkedIn profile can be just as important as having a great résumé? And, because it's public, your LinkedIn profile reaches a broader audience than submitting a résumé to an organization. Recruiters often use both during the hiring process—for recruiting but also for verification and validation. Discrepancies between a résumé and LinkedIn profile can raise red flags and be cause for concern. The good news is that once your résumé is complete, there is no need to create new experience content for your LinkedIn profile. But there is more to creating a LinkedIn profile. Here are key sections and some tips:

- **Close-up picture.** It could be a professional photo or a photo taken with your cell phone. Just include a plain background and wear a nice shirt.

- **Headline.** How do you want to be described? What are you excited about? Don't use a job title.

- **Summary.** Write in the first person, summarizing what motivates you, what you're skilled at, and what's next. Include an email address, relevant social media handles, and blog URL if appropriate.

- **Experience, Education, Honors & Awards.** This should match your résumé.

- **Skills & Expertise.** List at least five core skills and set up others to endorse you; start by endorsing others first to receive the return favor.

- **Recommendations.** Secure as many as you can from current and past contacts. Give direction to your recommenders so they know what to say about you. This bolsters your listed strengths and skills.

- **Custom URL.** Using your profile name, customizing the URL makes it easily shareable and avoids a long URL with random numbers.

- **Industry groups.** Based on your interests, join industry groups. Someone may check your digital profile to see if your claim of industry interest is true.

A cool benefit of LinkedIn is that you can upload content such as publications and videos. It's more dynamic than a flat résumé. And LinkedIn is a great tool for networking (more on that later)!

4. Elevator Pitch

How often do you get asked, "Tell me about yourself?" Your response to this question is an elevator pitch, which should be succinct and spark interest. It's called an elevator pitch because it shouldn't be longer than it takes to ride an elevator—about thirty to sixty seconds. An elevator pitch is important when networking or making professional introductions, attending career fairs, and interviewing for jobs. Elevator pitches are also used for sales and marketing meetings to promote ideas or products. Especially as you enter the job market, you need to be prepared by developing and perfecting your elevator pitch. Practice it with friends, in the mirror, or record it on your phone so that you can critique it and work out the kinks in your first draft.

Here are the key components:

- Introduce self (name).

- Explain what you do (relevant information such as school, major, internships, volunteer work, etc.).

- Explain what you want. (What is your ask? Is it to schedule a meeting to explore potential job opportunities, to make contacts within their business, or something else?)

The content matters but so does the delivery. Pay attention to your:

- **Cadence.** Are you talking too fast?

- **Clarity.** Are you speaking loud enough to be heard?

- **Tone.** Are you conveying confidence, warmth, seriousness, and so on?

- **Body language.** Are you making eye contact, smiling, paying attention to and engaging with others?

A great elevator pitch has all these components and, importantly, leads to an engaging conversation. Did you know there are even elevator pitch competitions?

What if you've reflected and prepared and are ready to take on the job market? Why not take the leap?

CHAPTER 2

LANDING YOUR FIRST JOB AFTER COLLEGE

Before landing your first job after college, you need to search for a job, apply, interview, and if you are offered the position, negotiate the job offer. This chapter covers these steps.

Job Search

This whole process takes time and patience. If you've heard the expression "searching for a job is a full-time job," it's because there is truth to it. Included below are the key components of searching for a job.

1. Utilize Your Informal Network

Every adult you know should be informed that you're in job search mode. Why? Because they might be able to help! Of course, in order for them to keep you in mind for a job opening, introduce you to others who might have relevant connections, or advocate for you in some way, they need to know what kind of role you're looking for. They probably know your character, and perhaps your professional interests, but do they know your skill set? Have they heard your elevator pitch? Have you shared your LinkedIn profile? Supply them with the kind of information they need in order to help you and keep them abreast during your job search, particularly as it relates to any assistance they have provided.

Because you are first-gen, not all of the adults in your life will have full knowledge of professional opportunities and steps in the process to get there. You may be surprised they have words of wisdom about forming and sustaining relationships and other things that are central to career success. At the same time, they will be on the learning journey with you. Welcome them.

2. Create and Maintain a List of Contacts

You will need to create and maintain a list of contacts. Otherwise, you might forget who you approached for what, what the next steps were going to be and whether you needed to reach back out, if you or they met a deadline, or if you sent a thank-you note to them. Use whatever format works best for you to create and maintain a list of contacts—Excel, Word, or on paper.

Some helpful categories to track are: name, title, organization, contact info, date(s) connected, original source for connection, key points from meeting, follow-up tasks /

responsibility / deadlines, and any other notes. The original source for connection is a category you may previously not have thought of. It's important because some contacts on your list will be based on referrals from others during your job search. Who referred you and the impact of their connection is something you'll want to follow up on with the person who originally made the introduction. This is a gesture of appreciation for sharing their network and is all too rare.

3. LAMP

LAMP is an acronym and job search approach from Steve Dalton's book, *The 2-Hour Job Search*, which I highly recommend. It is listed in the Resources section of this guidebook. LAMP stands for **l**ist, **a**dvocacy, **m**otivation, and **p**osting. I've slightly modified Steve's LAMP approach, which is described next.

List potential employers as the first step. How do you know which ones to list? Consider employers where your college alums work or who recruit on campus. Consider employers who you would dream to work for—perhaps you utilize their products or services and are a big fan. Consider employers who have posted ads and are actively recruiting. Consider employers who have been trending in the news for reasons you find interesting. Steve recommends listing forty employers. Whatever employers you list, make sure you do research on the organization before sorting and prioritizing as part of the LAMP process. Also follow them on social media.

Although the LAMP approach involves listing organizations, I suggest going deeper in researching the organizations.

Thoroughly research the job you're applying for—not just to get hired, but to make sure it's a good fit for you.

—Rachel Lloyd

Rachel is right. While you might not have a successful interview process without first doing research on the organization, imagine if you were offered and accepted the position and quickly learned it wasn't what you wanted. This would be a waste of everyone's time and money.

So what do you want to find out through your research? At the very least, you want to be able to state in your own words who their customers are, what market they are in (and how they make or raise money), and who their competitors are. Every organization, even nonprofits, have customers or clients, markets, and competitors. You probably also want to know about the mission, vision, and core values of the organization, as well as how your own values align. Then you need to think and state in your own words why you are interested in working at the organization.

Start your research by going to the organization's website and read the About Us section. If their annual report is included on their website, read that, too. Also conduct a general online search to see if they've been in the news and if so, why. You might want to look at Glassdoor and read employee reviews as well as consumer reviews on Yelp and ConsumerAffairs.

After researching the organization, the next part of LAMP involves estimating the probability of finding internal **advocates** at these organizations. You can rise above hundreds of applicants by having an internal advocate. Seventy-eighty percent of jobs are secured through personal networks[ii]. I'll discuss some options for how to find internal advocates in the **Informational Meetings** section of this handbook (described below).

Based on what you know about each of the forty employers, rate them on a scale of 1–3 (1 = low and 3 = high). What's your level of **motivation** in working with each employer? Reflect on why this is the case. It can help you gain insight. Motivation is the single most important factor in ranking your target employers. Why? Because it is a predictor of how engaged and committed you'll be in the workplace.

Finally, rate the relevance of the employer's job **posting** based on your skills, interests, and career goals. Give it a 3 if it's somewhat relevant, give it a 2 if it's not relevant, or give it a 1 if there is no job posting at all. Alternatively, you can rate each employer on your list with a job posting by using a different coding scheme that's meaningful to you.

Once you go through the LAMP approach, sort and prioritize the organizations for which you'll eventually apply.

4.   Informational Meetings

Requesting informational meetings is a great way to build rapport and gain useful information in your quest to find internal advocates. This is a key way to grow your network, which is particularly important for first-gen students who may not have a network that fully matches their career interests. Where do you start?

First, identify starter contacts for your top five organizations. Look for people who are in roles similar to the one for which you are applying or one or two levels above where you want to start. Perhaps they are fellow alumni, members of one of your affinity or LinkedIn groups (such as profession-specific communities like marketing or project management), or a weak tie (someone who you know but aren't in regular contact with, or a second-degree connection on LinkedIn). Join any and all alumni LinkedIn groups related to your interests. Try to aim for two or more contacts per organization. This will take some detective work, but in the process you will also be learning about the organization.

Second, connect with your identified contacts. If you share a LinkedIn group, you can message them directly for free through the group. If not through LinkedIn, find their email address and briefly (less than seventy-five words) write to them. In your written communication, state your connection first, then introduce yourself, and ask for insight/advice but not job leads. Define your interests both broadly and narrowly. Make your request to meet in the form of a question. Try and keep more than half of your word count about the contact and not about you. This is the advice from Steve Dalton and also advice I agree with. An example of an email introduction is below.

Hi [Contact's Name],

I came across your profile while researching [Company/Field], and your expertise in [specific area] stood out. I'm [Your Name], currently [your role/position] with an interest in [broad interest] and a focus on [narrow interest]. I'd value your perspective on navigating this field and your experience at [Company]. Would you be open to a brief conversation this week or next? I'd greatly appreciate your insights.

Best regards,

[Your Name]

Please know that not everyone will respond to your inquiry. Do track when you sent the message and any follow-up communication. After three business days, send a message or email to your second contact within the organization if you haven't heard back from the first contact. If you haven't heard from the first contact after seven days, send a reminder email. If there is no response after the next seven business days, move on. Use a similar process for each person you identified within the organization to contact. While this serial process is slower than a parallel process, it is more appropriate. Why? Because reaching out to multiple people in the same company at the same time could create confusion and give the impression that you're being overly aggressive or transactional. Plus, if one person within the company refers you to another, the introduction carries more weight than if you directly contacted that second person.

Third, when you do find a person within the organization to meet with for an informational meeting, the best outcome from a phone conversation, virtual meeting, or in-person meeting is to convince the contact to connect you directly to the organization. Between the first greeting and this best-scenario outcome, however, you want to have a successful meeting. Do your homework in advance (just like for an informational interview) and be ready to answer questions such as "Tell me about yourself" and "Why do you want to work for our organization, in this role, and in this industry (or sector)?" A twenty- to thirty-minute informational meeting should be structured as follows: (1) small talk (taking a genuine interest in the other person and asking follow-up questions), (2) move from small talk to Q&A on insights and trends (your questions on these matters should derive from your research, e.g., what do you attribute the 5 percent growth in market share to over the past six months? Do you see this trend continuing?), and (3) follow the insight and trend questions to questions that will benefit you. These can be advice, resources, or assignment questions (e.g., what advice would you give to someone like me who wants to work at your organization? Is there anyone else in your organization who you recommend I talk with to advance my application? What would you recommend I further research or learn about your organization or sector?). This helpful informational interview structure is further detailed in Steve Dalton's book *The 2-Hour Job Search*. Send a thank-you within twenty-four hours and follow up on any of your contact's recommendations within two weeks. Keep this contact updated at the two-week mark and then monthly (see Create and Maintain a List of Contacts above).

It's okay to say that you're first-gen. You may be pleasantly surprised to discover others who are in leadership roles who also started out as first-gen. Even if the person you are talking to isn't, they will likely appreciate this part of your identity.

While the best outcome is for this contact to advance your application internally, other outcomes could happen. For instance, you get advice, or you follow up and they continue the conversation via email. Another outcome is they don't respond after the two-week update email. If the latter is the case, ask a question. If still no response, move on. Appreciate what you've learned in the process.

5. Job Search Channels

The best advice has previously been provided because most jobs are found through networks, but don't forget to explore job boards (e.g., Indeed, Glassdoor, LinkedIn Jobs, Handshake, ZipRecruiter, etc.). In our survey, 35 percent of first-gen alums secured their first job through online job boards.

6. Campus Job Fairs and Recruiters

Have you been to a job fair on your campus? If not, check with your university's career services office to learn when job fairs take place and which organizations will have recruiters in attendance. This is an opportunity to use your elevator pitch, share your résumé, and learn more about potential organizations of interest. Dress as if you were attending a job interview; don't show up in the sweats you wore to class that day! You can also reach out to recruiters who specialize in your desired field. For example, type in terms like "recruiter," "talent acquisition specialist," or "headhunter" in the LinkedIn search followed by your target industry (e.g., "HR recruiter"). Once you've identified a recruiter, send a personalized message or email introducing yourself and your career goals, and attach your résumé for their review.

Applications

In addition to a cover letter and résumé, you might be asked to answer additional questions or take a test during the application process. These are ways to further screen potential candidates early on and before an interview.

HR Pro Tip

As a bonus, create business cards or QR codes to hand out during the fair. You may find connections within other attendees that may lead to other valuable connections or expand your network in general.

Extra Questions

Sometimes an online application process includes an extra step: answering questions. This is before a potential screening interview. Why? Because the organization wants to know a bit more about you before taking the time to interview you. You don't need to answer these questions immediately. Be strategic in thinking about your responses and then log back in once you're ready to answer the questions.

Typically, these questions fall into three categories: (1) getting to know you, (2) cultural fit with the organization, and (3) skills. For example: What attracted you to this specific role? What values are important to you in the workplace and why? What is an example of how you've used a specific tool, platform, or technique in a past role? As with answering any questions, be honest, concise, and specific to the role and organization.

You might also be required to list your expected salary. Salary ranges and text (not numbers) are often not allowed in those fields. It's important that you know the appropriate salary for the targeted position in that particular geographic region before answering this question. Glassdoor.com, Salary.com, and Payscale.com are three online resources that provide salary by job title for companies and/or geographic regions.

Tests

Depending on the industry, organizational requirements, and role, the job application process may require one or more tests. These tests help employers evaluate a candidate's fit for a role in terms of skill and personality. For example, there are aptitude tests that measure general reasoning, problem-solving, and the ability to learn and adapt. There are tests to evaluate specific skills required for a job, such as coding and editing. There are also psychometric and personality tests to assess personality traits and behaviors that align with job requirements.

Sometimes tests are job simulation exercises that provide a realistic preview through practice exercises resembling tasks in the actual role. There are also case study interviews often used by consulting firms, finance roles, and management positions. Researching the types of tests used by specific organizations and preparing in advance can help increase your chances of success.

Interviews

When applying and interviewing, always speak on how you can add value to the organization or team rather than why you want the job.

—Cassandra Skenandore

If you did your research on the organization and created a résumé addendum that matches the job description to your knowledge, skills, and experience, you'll be in good shape for the interview. The interviewer wants to know you understand the job, you can do the job, and you want the job. So make sure you show enthusiasm. Also make sure to shake hands and look people in the eye.

> **HR Pro Tip**
>
> *Think of each phase of the interview as a time to shine. Be yourself and remember the value you bring.*

There are different types of interviews. There's the screening interview that could be over the phone or virtual, and it is brief (fifteen to thirty minutes). The purpose is to determine if basic qualifications are met and if there's a good fit for the position. If you advance to a second round of interviews, it could be one-on-one, with a panel (typically two to five people interview one candidate), or in a group (more than one candidate is interviewed at the same time by one or more interviewers), virtual or in-person. Sometimes there are multiple rounds, and these interviews could be thirty minutes or longer. At some point in the process, you'll interview with the hiring manager, the person who will make the hiring decision. It's always good to know about the person or people you'll be interviewing with in advance of the interview. At the very least, review their LinkedIn profile. It should help you feel more comfortable, and you might discover things you have in common.

There's one part of the interview you can pretty much nail down in advance—your personal pitch. I'll describe it first (though it will not be the first thing you say in an interview; most likely you'll give your personal pitch near the closing of the interview). I'll then identify tactics for responding to common interview questions.

Cassandra's quote above is key in preparing your personal pitch. You need to understand the organization, your role, your skill set, and clearly and concisely explain what value you would add to the organization. After you explain your value, include why this position is perfect for you. Here's an example:

Your commitment to leveraging data to enhance [specific organization initiative or value] is something I am passionate to help advance. I will eagerly contribute my skills in data analysis and statistical modeling and enthusiastically serve on your team. In addition to my technical skills, you'll find I bring a fresh perspective, learn quickly, and I pride myself on translating technical findings into meaningful stories for diverse audiences, which from our conversation, I know is a priority for [specific organization].

Here are a two general categories of interview questions (with a few examples) and some strategies to help you prepare effectively:

General Background and Fit. Can you tell me about yourself? What attracted you to [Organization Name]? You'll be prepared to answer these questions with your elevator pitch and having researched the organization, as noted earlier in this chapter.

Behavioral Questions. Tell me a time you failed at something. What did you learn from it? Describe a time you had to learn a new skill or tool quickly. How did you do it? Use the STAR framework to answer these types of behavioral questions. Here's an example.

Situation

During my final semester in college, I was part of a group project where we needed to analyze a large dataset and present actionable insights to the professor.

Task

One of my key tasks was to ensure that all team members contributed their parts on time so we could review and refine the final report before the presentation. However, I underestimated how long it would take to consolidate everyone's work and double-check the accuracy of our findings.

Action

As the presentation on the report approached, I realized we didn't have enough time to thoroughly review our analysis. I took it upon myself to merge all the sections quickly but missed some inconsistencies in the data. During the presentation, the professor pointed out a significant error in our analysis, which impacted our grade. Afterward, I spoke with my team to identify what went wrong and reflected on my approach.

Result

Although the experience was humbling, it taught me a lesson— the importance of realistic planning. I now build in extra time for reviews and account for unexpected delays in project timelines. Since then, I've applied this lesson to projects, including [specific project], where our team delivered high-quality results ahead of schedule.

For more in-depth information on interviews, check out Amy Feind Reeves's book *College to Career Explained* (chapter 11, "Acing the Interview") and Brittany Danielle's brief but highly accessible eBook *The Ultimate Interview Guide*. (Both are listed in the Resources section of this guidebook.)

With in-person interviews, make sure you have copies of your résumé and any show-and-tell items (e.g., writing samples if the position requires writing). A "kudos" file is recommended by Brittany Danielle. She recommends copying and pasting any notes of recognition for your accomplishments from colleagues in one file that you can print out and bring with you to an interview. Another high-impact document to include in your file is a draft 30-60-90-day plan for the position for which you are applying. This document highlights what you would do within the first ninety days of being hired and will set you apart from other candidates. An abbreviated example follows.

DRAFT

30-60-90-Day Plan for Assist. Dean Student Services and Programs

Prepared by: Jane Doe

Prepared for: Jane Smith

Focus	Priority Tasks	30 Day	60 Day	90 Day
Orientation	• Organizational chart review	X		
	• Strategic plan review	X		
	• Department-wide initiatives review	X		
	• Budgets review		X	
	• Operations mapping	X		
Trust Building	Students			
	• Meet 1:1 or small group with student leaders	X	X	X
	• Attend events	X	X	X
	• Small group coffee/tea monthly sessions	X	X	X
	College academic and program leadership, and support staff	X	X	X
	Campus and community resources		X	X

Mitigating Risk	Title IX			
	• Process review	X		
	• Training	X	X	X
	• Historical analysis		X	X
	• Lateral knowledge sharing		X	X
	• Hot-button issues	X	X	X
Data Analytics	Metrics and dashboards			
	• Students, degree programs			X
	• Assess policy implementation			X
	• Predictive analytics			X
Events, Initiatives, Products	• Orientation	X		
	• Commencement		X	X
	• High-profile speakers		X	X

Finally, don't forget to send a thank-you note to everyone you met during the interview. Do this within twenty-four hours. Write something specific and unique that you appreciated during the interview and reiterate your interest in the position. An example follows.

Dear [Interviewer's Name],

Thank you for taking the time to speak with me about the [Position Name] role at [Company] yesterday. I truly appreciated the opportunity to learn more about your team and the exciting projects you're working on, particularly [specific topic discussed, e.g., the upcoming launch of the new product line].

Our conversation reinforced my enthusiasm for joining your team and contributing my [specific skill/experience] to [specific goal or project]. Please let me know if there's any additional information I can provide.

Thank you again for your time and insights. I look forward to the possibility of working together.

Best regards,

[Your Full Name]

[Your Contact Information]

References

If you are progressing along in the interview process and are a finalist, employers will want you to list at least one reference. This usually includes the name, phone number, and email of your reference and perhaps a word or two about how long you have known them or in what capacity. Why are references important? Because people who serve as references can provide a perspective on your skills, character, and work history. For the employer, it mitigates against risk in hiring. For instance, if you list a former supervisor as a reference, they can validate your dates of employment and other information you list on your résumé. Whether it's a former employer, a work colleague, or a professor, include someone on your reference list who can provide a good character evaluation. This helps employers determine if you're a good cultural fit for their organization.

It's important to know that strong, credible references can differentiate you from other candidates. Remember that! As such, make sure your references know you well and can enthusiastically speak about your candidacy.

Here are some tips when asking someone to serve as a reference for you.

- Ask them in advance of listing them as a reference. While you can do this over email, it's more impactful to have a two-way conversation over the phone or virtually if you can't do so in person. Share with them your résumé and cover letter and/or LinkedIn profile. Let them know the position(s) you are applying for and why you would like for them to serve as a reference. Is it because they can speak to your work ethic? Is it because they can speak on behalf of your character in that they've known you for a long time? Is it because they can speak to how you're a fast learner or team player? Think of the reasons why you are asking them to serve and express to them the reason(s) why it's important to you. Provide them with a hyperlink to the organization.

- Don't forget to thank them for their time in serving as a reference. Also, be sure to circle back to your references to let them know the actual outcome of your job interview process. Doing so will make it less awkward if you need to ask them to serve as a reference for you again in the future.

Negotiating a Job Offer

Many parts of a job offer are negotiable—likely more than you realize.

Even before you have an offer, start with a personal inventory. Do you like to negotiate? Are you good at asking for things? Do you stand up to people in authority? Many people would say no to these questions—bargaining feels uncomfortable or worse. It might be helpful for you to know that employers are actually expecting you to negotiate with them!

It turns out there are many things you can do to increase your confidence and increase your likelihood of success. In negotiations, the most important thing to do is prepare. Here are some ways to do that:

1. **Make a list of your hopes, fears, and concerns.** This might include opportunities to learn, make a difference, or improve your standard of living. Know what is important to you when it comes to a job.

2. **Do the same thing for the organization.** What might

> **HR Pro Tip**
>
> *Paid time off, professional memberships, work conferences, and other fringe benefits can be negotiated and offered in lieu of salary increases.*

be their hopes, fears, and concerns with you? Know that you represent next-generation talent for them. Be bold and identify five ways you can add value to the organization from its point of view.

3. **Do your homework.** It might be hard to find out exactly what would be the salary for a job you've been offered, but there are ways to get an idea of the likely range on sites like Glassdoor.com, Salary.com, and Payscale. com.

4. **Make a list of things that could be negotiable with a full-time job.** These include initial assignments, moving costs, a review in six months (rather than a year), the start date, a signing bonus (especially if there is not much room to move on salary), and starting salary. At the very least, ask for a salary that will be fair relative to others doing similar work.

All of this is preparation work. When it comes to meeting and actually negotiating, here is some guidance:

1. **Say thank you to the offer, no matter what the offer is.** Then get a pencil and paper and indicate that you want to write it down. You will look forward to the written offer but you want to learn all you can now. Write down all the information they share with you.

2. **In response, don't focus first on salary.** Instead ask questions about the work, such as your likely initial

assignment, supervisory responsibilities, and committee work.

3. **Even if you plan to accept the position, don't do so immediately.** If the organization is your first choice, say so but also inform them that you don't want to officially accept until you have had a chance to study their proposal and get back to them.

When you think about job negotiations, you most likely think salary. I understand why that would be at the top of your negotiating list. Let's say they make a salary offer or ask about your salary expectations. An appropriate response would be one in which you say that based on what you presently know about the position and their geographical area, the salary range for such a job is [$$$ to $$$]. It is okay to say you are expecting to come in at the high end of the range and, in any case, you would like to be paid fairly, relative to other people doing similar work.

Ask questions rather than make demands. Are there options around your initial assignment? If there's no option to increase the salary, can there be a signing bonus and coverage of moving expenses?

What if you have multiple offers?

If you have multiple offers, don't play them off against each other. You can say you have a higher offer from another organization, but they are not your first choice. As such, you are hoping a salary can be agreed to that both of you are comfortable with.

If you accept a written offer, inform other organizations where you have pending applications so they can continue with their hiring process. If you accept a written offer and later receive an offer from another organization that is more appealing, you should proceed in an ethical way by declining the second offer. You can always pursue employment there in the future if you desire to do so. Although there are exceptions, in most cases an offer and acceptance of that offer is expected to be honored by both parties. Always ask to receive a written contractual agreement to ensure clarity regarding your job title, general expectations, salary, start date, and other negotiated matters.

In conclusion, throughout the negotiation process, keep in mind your initial analysis of your interests and theirs. Be clear about what is and isn't important to you, and ask questions if you need clarification on any aspect of the job.

In the end, you can turn what may initially seem like a stressful negotiation into a joint problem-solving exercise where you both feel good about the final outcome.

Imagine, what if all your preparation and persistence leads you to the perfect role? Why not make it yours?

CHAPTER 3

COMMON PERSONAL BARRIERS

By Annalea Forrest, MPH, MSW, ACSW

Being a first-generation college graduate is not just a personal achievement—it's a testament to your adaptability, determination, and perseverance. Employers value the unique strengths you bring: problem-solving skills honed through navigating uncharted paths, resourcefulness developed from overcoming systemic challenges, and an unparalleled work ethic driven by deep personal and familial motivation. You've learned to bridge cultural gaps, advocate for yourself in unfamiliar environments, and persevere through obstacles that might discourage others. These qualities make you not just a great employee but a leader and a change maker. Your lived experience has prepared you to adapt, learn quickly, and connect with diverse teams—skills employers seek but can't teach. The challenges you've faced in life are not setbacks; they're proof of your strength. Recognizing these strengths and embracing your worth are crucial parts of navigating your career successfully and evolving as a professional with confidence.

Yet, despite these strengths, it's easy as first-generation college graduates to internalize struggles as a reflection of our capabilities or our value, often because we have experienced navigating these struggles alone or with criticism. When the road feels especially tough, it might seem like we're struggling because we're the problem—that somehow we're inherently lacking the necessary things it takes to overcome our struggles or barriers. But here's the reality: the barriers we experience are not reflections of our inherent worth or capability to succeed. When we refer to *personal barriers* in this chapter, we're referring to the struggles faced by you, a first-generation college grad, that are unique and intimate and impactful to you as a particular person. These barriers, if not overcome, can become barriers to you thriving in careers and other life stages. Many of these personal barriers you face are *not* your fault, and just because these struggles are personal and particular to *you* does not mean you can or are expected to overcome them alone. The barriers discussed in this chapter are meant to be overcome through the development of self-knowledge and self-advocacy, and with interpersonal and community support. We can't fully overcome these particular barriers alone—and to all you resilient first-generation college grads out there, that was not meant to be taken as a challenge!

One way to reframe our perspective on our ability to overcome personal barriers is to distinguish between personal *attributes* and personal *barriers*. Personal attributes are qualities that shape our personhood, like our personality and social identities (such as gender, ethnicity, cultural background, education level, income group, or ability status). Personal barriers, on the other hand, are obstacles we encounter relevant to our personal attributes and because of our circumstances or environment. For example, you might be a highly motivated student (a personal attribute), but you could still struggle with time management as you're balancing school, work, and family responsibilities (a personal barrier). By distinguishing between who we are and what we're facing, we can start to see the barriers as challenges that can be overcome rather than as flaws within ourselves.

The personal barriers discussed in this chapter are not caused by your personality factors or social identities. It is disempowering to blame your gender, culture, or family education as the barrier to success rather than to blame things that can be changed, such as the presence of unjust biases and lack of support. The personal barriers discussed in this chapter largely stem from historical and remaining oppressive policies and treatment rooted in the effort to restrict access to financial, educational, and health resources for people who are working class, non-White, non-male, and have any type of disability. Although there are more protections in the modern workplace for people of protected classes such as those listed above, first-generation college grads still face personal barriers related to overcoming policies and treatment that do not consider the needs or uplift the lived experiences of people who are overcoming oppression.

First-generation college grads may experience these barriers as uniquely difficult due to being among the first in our family to graduate college and pursue a career. As a college graduate, not only do you have access to opportunities that were not previously available to the older generations of your family, but you may be now navigating those opportunities feeling a little isolated and with different skills and support than peers who come from college-educated families have. It's normal to feel intimidated when facing new challenges, but before you doubt your ability to face these personal barriers while you navigate starting your career, it's important to recognize that overcoming these personal barriers is not a deterrence from your chosen life path or career. The very acts of facing these personal barriers and bridging any knowledge and skill gaps are actually the stepping stones on the path to growth and success on your life path and career. Most importantly, you'll be taking every step with your resolve and unique perspective, which will take you further on your path than you might imagine.

While facing personal barriers can feel overwhelming, it's also an opportunity for growth. Each time we navigate a challenge, we're building skills, resilience, and a stronger sense of self. The very act of confronting these barriers is part of our development. In this way, personal barriers are not just obstacles—they are an integral part of the path to success. The journey of overcoming barriers is not one we have to walk alone, even if we're used to solving problems independently. As first-generation college graduates, many of us have developed a strong sense of self-reliance out of necessity. However, it's essential to remember that seeking support is a strength, not a weakness. By reaching out for help, whether it's from mentors or peers, we can gain new perspectives and strategies to tackle the challenges we face. Together, we can transform these barriers into opportunities for growth and success.

This chapter identifies six common barriers first-generation college graduates experience in the initial and early stages of their careers. The last portion of the chapter identifies high-impact exercises, tools, and related resources for addressing these barriers.

1. Family Dynamics

Your family may be immensely proud and yet have no idea how to contribute or support you because they've never experienced this.

—April M.

Have you ever felt torn between two worlds—one you've worked so hard to enter and another that feels like home? For many first-generation college graduates, transitioning to our job after graduation can bring up unique challenges rooted in family dynamics.

This experience can be both rewarding and challenging. There can be a mix of unspoken expectations, competing cultural values, and feelings of guilt or pressure. How can you move forward in your career while staying connected to the family that helped you get there?

First, it's important to recognize that families often play a unique role in the lives of first-generation graduates. For many, family is more than just support; it's an anchor. However, starting a new job—especially one in a field unfamiliar to your family—can create a gap in understanding and connection. Have you ever tried explaining your new role or schedule, only to feel like they don't quite get it? It is further complicated since parts of the new role—what you should or should not do—are still not fully clear to you. This can leave you feeling isolated or even unsure about whether you're making the right choices.

Second, a common challenge is the expectation to give back financially, as further discussed in chapter 5. Many first-generation graduates come from families where supporting one another is a core value, and earning a paycheck may come with an unspoken duty to contribute. This can lead to stress when you're trying to balance paying your bills, managing student loans, and building your future. How do you explain that you're not yet in a position to give as much as you'd like? It can feel like you're letting your family down, even when you're doing your best.

Third, guilt is another emotional hurdle. Have you ever felt like you were leaving your family behind as you climbed higher? Being the first to achieve a college degree and enter a professional world can come with the weight of being a trailblazer. Some graduates may feel pressure to stay connected by limiting their opportunities or downplaying their successes to avoid creating distance.

So what can you do to manage these dynamics while staying true to yourself? Start by opening up conversations with your family. Sharing what you're going through—your hopes, your challenges, and even your fears—can help them see the bigger picture. Could setting clear boundaries help, too? For example, letting your family know when you're available to help versus when you need to focus on your job. You may even find that members of your family have encountered and addressed their own trailblazing challenges—ones that you were not aware of.

Remember, you're not alone in facing these barriers, and you're not failing because it feels hard. Growing into a new role while maintaining your family connections is a balancing act—but one that many others have successfully navigated. Your journey is a testament to your hard work and resilience, and in time, you'll find ways to bridge the gap. After all, isn't this transition proof of just how far you've come?

2. Imposter Syndrome

Imposter syndrome is REAL. It was so helpful to have my supervisor support me through times where I encountered a lot of internal uncertainty.

Had it not been for my supervisor, I would not have thrived as much as I did.

—Miguel H.

Have you ever felt like Miguel? You know that feeling when you're doing something important and this little voice in your head starts saying, *It's only a matter of time before everyone realizes you're not as capable as they think?* No matter how much you achieve, you have this nagging doubt that maybe you just got lucky, or maybe you somehow tricked people into thinking what you're capable of doing. It's this constant inner struggle between wanting to believe in yourself and being convinced you'll be discovered as a fraud. That's imposter syndrome.

The concept was first introduced as imposter phenomena almost fifty years ago. When it became highly popularized through social media, the term morphed from imposter phenomena to imposter syndrome, at which point it inaccurately became viewed as a pathology instead of an experience. It's now recognized as affecting people of all genders. It is often tied to perfectionism, cultural expectations, or when you feel unprepared and out of place. You can imagine how it can be especially prevalent with first-generation college graduates, as we are in new spaces and places. We often can feel like we don't belong.

But imposter syndrome is not without criticism because it unfairly places the burden of self-doubt and inadequacy on individuals. It doesn't address the systemic barriers (such as gender bias and racial inequities) that contribute to these feelings, particularly for women of color.

You are not in any of these places by accident. You're there on purpose...that means you deserve to be there.

—Shanicka S. Burdine

If you feel like Miguel, take heart in Shanicka's advice. As hard as it might be sometimes, try to remind yourself that your feelings don't define your worth or your abilities. They are not facts, just feelings that will pass. It is not a pathology! Consider the broader systemic barriers that could also be factors contributing to how you're feeling. And keep track of your accomplishments and accolades as reminders for when you're feeling the imposter syndrome voice talking to you.

3. Systemic Barriers

I was the only person of color on my immediate HR team and that felt like such an unfortunate continuation of college and being in professional spaces where you don't feel you belong.

—April M.

Have you ever looked around at your new job and thought, *I don't really belong here?* If you have, you're not alone. Many first-generation college graduates don't just experience imposter syndrome—the feeling that you've only achieved success by luck, not because of your own abilities—but also encounter new systemic barriers.

For first-generation graduates, entering professional spaces often means stepping into environments that weren't designed with them in mind. Have you ever noticed that many of your coworkers come from wealthier backgrounds, have family connections in the field, or share similar experiences that you don't? These differences can make you feel out of place, as if you're the exception rather than someone who rightfully earned their spot. This isn't just a personal feeling—it's a result of systems that have historically excluded people like you.

Imagine being the only person of your background, culture, or identity in the room. Do you ever feel pressure to prove you deserve to be there? When you don't see others like yourself in leadership roles or even among your peers, it's easy to internalize the idea that you're not enough. But here's the truth: the problem isn't you—it's the systems that have made these spaces inaccessible for so long.

Microaggressions and stereotypes also contribute to feelings of not belonging. Have you ever had someone question your qualifications or make a comment that undermines your success? These subtle but harmful messages can plant seeds of doubt, making you second-guess your abilities even when you've worked just as hard (or harder) than anyone else. The constant need to prove yourself can take a toll, leaving you feeling like you'll never measure up—even when you already do.

So how can you combat these feelings when they are tied to larger systems? Start by reframing your perspective. Instead of asking yourself, *Do I belong here?*, ask yourself, *Why wouldn't I belong here?* You've earned your success through dedication, talent, and perseverance. The fact that you're breaking barriers is a testament to your strength, not a sign that you don't fit.

It's also important to challenge the systems that make you feel this way. Surround yourself with people who understand your journey, whether it's coworkers, mentors, or peers who share similar experiences. Have you thought about joining professional groups for first-generation graduates or people from your background? Finding a supportive community can remind you that you're not alone and your perspective adds value to your workplace.

Finally, remember that the presence of bias doesn't diminish your worth. Instead of focusing on the ways you feel different, celebrate the unique skills and insights you bring to the table. The very things that make you stand out are what make you a valuable part of your team.

The feelings may feel personal, but they are often rooted in larger systems that weren't built to include everyone. By recognizing these influences, you can start to reclaim your confidence and understand that you *do* belong. Isn't it time to trust in the same strength that got you here? You've already proven yourself—you just need to believe it.

4. Encountering Institutional Knowledge

One of the significant challenges I faced in my first role was understanding how to approach the assigned tasks and overcoming the fear of reporting any challenges I encountered. Initially, I felt pressured to complete assignments without encountering any obstacles. However, I quickly learned the importance of seeking clarification and assistance when needed. I realized that asking questions, reaching out to unfamiliar colleagues within the organization, and addressing issues openly with the entire team were essential steps in overcoming challenges effectively. This shift in mindset enabled me to foster collaboration, gain valuable insights from diverse perspectives, and ultimately enhance my problem-solving skills. Embracing open communication and seeking support from colleagues proved instrumental in navigating through complex tasks and achieving successful outcomes.

—Keshav Regmi

Have you ever started a job and felt like everyone else knew a secret playbook that you didn't? For first-generation college graduates, stepping into our first job can feel like entering a completely foreign world. From unspoken office norms to hidden rules about networking, the lack of institutional knowledge—the informal know-how that others take for granted—can make the transition feel overwhelming. How do you figure it all out when no one has taught you the rules?

Institutional knowledge isn't something we learn in a classroom. It's the implicit and explicit advice and insights often passed down from family members or mentors who've been in similar roles or have experience in professional organizations. Have you ever heard someone talk about "working the system" or "office politics" and wondered what that actually means? Many first-generation graduates come from families where professional careers are uncharted territory, leaving us to navigate these unwritten rules on our own.

Take workplace culture, for example. Do you know when it's okay to speak up in meetings or how to ask for help without seeming unprepared? For those who haven't been exposed to professional environments, figuring out these dynamics can feel like walking a tightrope. Small things— like how to write a professional email or how to approach your boss—might seem obvious to others but can be a source of stress for someone learning on the fly.

Networking is another part of institutional knowledge that can be intimidating. Have you ever wondered how people form connections that seem to open doors for new opportunities? Many first-generation graduates don't have the family or social networks others rely on to get ahead. Building those relationships from scratch can feel daunting, especially when you're not sure where to start or what to say.

So how can you navigate this lack of institutional knowledge while still thriving in your first job? Start by reminding yourself that it's okay not to know everything right away. Have you ever considered that asking questions is actually a strength, not a weakness? Showing curiosity and a willingness to learn can help you gain the insights you need over time.

As you'll see in chapter 4, finding a mentor can also be a game changer. Is there someone at work you admire or who seems approachable? Many people are happy to share advice if you ask, and having someone to guide you can help you fill in the gaps that institutional knowledge leaves behind.

Finally, give yourself grace. Everyone's first job is a learning experience, and no one expects you to have all the answers on day one. The fact that you're willing to grow and adapt already sets you apart. Isn't navigating this unfamiliar territory proof of your resilience and determination?

You're not alone in feeling like you're figuring things out as you go. With time, effort, and a little patience, you'll build the knowledge and confidence to succeed—not just in this job but in every step of your career. After all, isn't learning part of the journey that makes success so rewarding?

5. Chronic Stress and Burnout

I was overworking for so long and extremely burned out. I used to get to work around 7:00 a.m. and leave around 6:00 p.m. I would then work more at home in the evening. I also worked on weekends as well. I barely had a life outside of work. The pressure from my employer to keep ramping up productivity was so difficult. Especially given the depression and loneliness that I experienced at that time during my first job.

—Manuel Gomez

Can you relate to Manuel? Do you feel the pressure to perform at work to provide for yourself while adjusting to new environments, roles, and social expectations?

As first-generation college graduates, we often face a unique set of challenges that can quietly build over time, leading to chronic stress—and eventually, burnout. Have you ever felt like you're juggling too many things at once for an extended period of time and there's just no room to catch your breath? That's chronic stress. It's not just a tough week; it's an unrelenting weight that makes even the simplest tasks feel like climbing a mountain.

Burnout, on the other hand, is what happens when your chronic stress doesn't get managed. It's that bone-deep exhaustion where you're running on empty, feeling detached, and like you'll never catch up. Burnout is a type of stress injury, and its effects are similar to an athlete who becomes strained during athletic performance. Imagine running a marathon without water or rest—at some point, they're bound to hit a wall. Those runners don't just jump back up and keep going after some water or a quick break—they're out for the race. For many of us first-generation graduates, the constant pressure of balancing expectations leaves little time to recover, and without rest, it's easy to lose the resilience needed to keep going.

It may feel familiar or intuitive to put your nose to the grindstone and keep hustling until your employer and/or bank account is satisfied. But here's the tricky part: when we're in that go-go-go mindset or in a constant state of survival, it's hard to pause, let alone intentionally choose something that refuels us. Have you ever had the thought, *If I stop right now, I don't know if I'll be able to start again* or *I don't have time to slow down or even* do *self-care right now*?

The struggle to pause when we're in a state of go-go-go is called productivity inertia—the idea that, like objects in motion, we stay in motion until an outside force literally *forces* us to stop. It's true that if we don't manage stress, our stress will manage us. If we keep going day-to-day without real awareness of just how stressed or overwhelmed we are, or without a daily practice of healthy stress management techniques, we end up like an overstretched rubber band with our unmanaged stress waiting to snap back and grab our attention through external cues of sickness, depression, and burnout. You may be capable of incredible things under pressure, but humans are not machines!

During stressful times, it's important to focus on what you can control. One way to do this is by managing your energy with healthy habits, like sleep, exercise, good food, spending time with others, and getting proper rest. It's also important to have a daily routine that includes both stress prevention and stress intervention. Stress prevention helps lower stress before it builds up by doing things like deep breathing, staying organized, getting support from others, and taking breaks. Stress intervention helps you deal with high stress by completing the stress cycle and avoiding burnout.

While chronic stress can be managed with prevention and intervention, burnout is different. Burnout isn't managed— it's healed. Burnout happens when you've been under too much strain for too long, and healing takes both strain recovery and stress management together.

The examples set by parents, siblings, elders, and others may or may not help. We may have absorbed messages that emphasize overworking, achievement, hyperproductivity, and deprioritizing rest, for example. In these cases, there is the assumption that all this intensity will help us feel in control and give us a fulfilling sense of managing our responsibilities. However, without intentional rest, recovery, and play, that approach usually leads to deep physical and emotional exhaustion, a lack of fulfillment, loneliness, and even chronic illness or debilitation.

So how do you know when to pause or what you need in order to recover? The key lies in understanding your personal stress signals and what helps you bounce back. Managing stress isn't one-size-fits-all; it's both an art and a science. Sure, there are foundational practices like setting boundaries, staying present, and managing your time, but effective stress management is also deeply personal. What works for you might change from day-to-day—and that's okay. This personal approach to reducing stress in our lives is what people often refer to when they reference "self-care." See recommendations for managing chronic stress and addressing burnout (later in this chapter).

6. Mental Health Challenges

Have you ever felt like the excitement of reaching a milestone was clouded by an undercurrent of worry or sadness? For many first-generation college graduates, stepping into their first job after graduation is a proud accomplishment, yet it often comes with unseen mental health challenges. Anxiety, depression, and even unresolved trauma can create barriers that make this transition even harder. How can you focus on building your career while carrying these emotional weights?

Let's start with anxiety. Adjusting to a new work environment can feel overwhelming for anyone, but for first-generation graduates, it can feel like the stakes are even higher. Do you ever catch yourself thinking, *What if I fail? What if I'm not good enough?* These thoughts can trigger a cycle of overthinking and self-doubt. From worrying about fitting in with colleagues to navigating workplace expectations, anxiety can make even small challenges feel like towering hurdles.

Depression can also creep in during this time, often fueled by isolation or the weight of high expectations. Have you ever felt a deep sadness, even when things seem to be going well on the surface? Depression might make you feel disconnected from others or unmotivated to perform tasks you used to enjoy. For first-generation graduates, the pressure to succeed and make our family proud can compound these feelings, leaving us stuck between exhaustion and guilt.

Trauma adds another layer of complexity. Some first-generation graduates come from backgrounds where we've faced financial hardship, discrimination, or instability. Some of us have experienced past violence, homelessness, and food insecurity. Do you ever feel like old memories resurface during stressful times? Trauma can make it harder to adapt to new environments, as unresolved experiences might trigger feelings of fear, insecurity, or unworthiness. The professional world often emphasizes confidence and composure, which can feel out of reach when we're struggling internally.

How can we manage anxiety, depression, or trauma when cultural norms discourage us from addressing mental health challenges? In many cultures, mental health is not openly discussed, and seeking support can be seen as a sign of weakness or failure. Have you ever felt like asking for help might lead to judgment or disappointment? For first-generation graduates, cultural stigma can make it even harder to prioritize our well-being during the transition to a new job.

Start by understanding that self-care is not selfish—it's survival. In cultures where sacrifice and hard work are often seen as the only acceptable paths to success, carving out time to care for yourself may feel indulgent or even shameful. But have you ever considered how small acts of self-care, like a moment of silence to breathe or a walk to clear your mind, can restore your energy and focus? Even within the constraints of cultural expectations, finding ways to nurture yourself is a powerful act of resistance and resilience.

Professional support, while essential, can be challenging to pursue in the face of cultural stigma. Have you ever heard phrases like, "You just need to be strong" or "Mental health issues aren't real problems"? These attitudes can discourage first-generation graduates from reaching out to therapists, counselors, or support groups. But seeking professional help is not a sign of failure—it's an investment in your future. Finding a culturally competent therapist who understands your background can make the process feel more comfortable and less isolating.

HR Pro Tip

Many employers offer employee assistance Programs (EAP) that include a set number of free counseling sessions with a therapist.

Community care offers another pathway to healing, especially in cultures where family and community are central to identity. Who in your circle might be open to supporting you, even if mental health isn't a topic they usually discuss? It can help to frame conversations around shared values, like strength, perseverance, and the desire to succeed. Saying something like, "Talking to someone will help me stay strong and achieve my goals" might resonate with loved ones who otherwise view mental health concerns skeptically. By finding common ground, you can slowly break down stigma and build understanding.

As you navigate anxiety, depression, or trauma, remember that cultural stigma doesn't have to dictate your journey. Yes, it can feel like an uphill battle to prioritize your mental health when doing so goes against the grain, but your well-being is worth the effort. By practicing self-care, seeking professional support, and leaning on your community in ways that work for you, you can overcome these challenges. Isn't your strength in breaking barriers proof that you're capable of facing anything that comes your way? You've already defied expectations to reach this point, and you deserve the space to care for yourself—without guilt or shame.

Turning Barriers into Building Blocks

You've read about the barriers that first-generation college graduates often encounter; now it's time to turn insight into action. The activities listed below are designed to be high-impact and help you address each barrier with practical steps that fit into your life. Remember, overcoming challenges doesn't mean fixing yourself—it means finding tools that work for you.

Each of these activities offer a practical way to address barriers while building confidence and resilience. You don't need to tackle everything at once.

What if you focused on just one small step to spark positive change? Why not embrace what works for you and trust the process of growth?

Family Dynamics

Activity: Connection Rituals and Value Alignment

Create intentional connection rituals like regular calls or visits to express the value of your relationships. Share your journey in relatable terms to help your family understand your choices. Additionally, engage in a values clarification exercise—write down personal and family values to find areas of overlap. Reflecting on this overlap can help you feel connected to your family while pursuing your career.

Activity: Setting Compassionate Boundaries

> *Boundaries are the distance at which I can love you and me simultaneously.*
>
> —Prentis Hemphill, psychotherapist

Boundaries are the way we enable ourselves to meet our own needs while simultaneously exercising our ability to show up for others in loving, supportive ways. Boundaries are tools that are designed to help us while sharing with others within our capacity so that we are able to sustainably support ourselves and others. Boundaries keep relation-ships, but walls (rigid, inflexible rules) keep them out.

This tool can help you set boundaries—at work or with loved ones—in a way that protects the relationship while keeping you feeling safe and respected. The culturally responsive DEAR MAN framework (**d**escribe, **e**xpress, **a**ssert, **r**einforce, **m**indful, **a**ppear confident, **n**egotiate) allows you to be kind but firm.

For example, if a family member is facing a financial emergency and needs support, you may want to help but aren't comfortable giving money. Setting a boundary with empathy and cultural awareness is key. Every culture has different implicit expectations for support, and balancing your family's need with your own is both important and healthy. Validating their feelings while ensuring your ac-tions are sustainable for both of you creates a stronger, healthier dynamic.

Describe: "I understand you're going through a tough time right now and need some extra support."

Express: "I care about you, but unfortunately I'm not in a position to give financial support right now. It's not some-thing I can afford to do without impacting my own financial responsibilities but I can. . ."

Assert: "What I could do is help you with _____[fill in the blank of what you can offer, like budgeting or exploring other potential resources]."

Reinforce: "I know this is difficult and I care about you so much, and I'm willing to help through listening or finding a longer-term solution that could really help you down the road. I'm here to help in _____ ways since I'm unable to provide_____ or I'm unable to directly provide money."

While this is a script that can be used, many conversations require nuance, presence, and the ability to navigate difficult emotions. While in conversation, be mindful. For example, if the family member replies, "I really need it now," calmly reiterate "I understand, but I'm unable to because _____ but I can do _____."

Appear confident by maintaining a warm tone, such as "This isn't about not wanting to help—I just have to manage my own responsibilities carefully right now."

Negotiate alternatives, showing that you're willing to help in other ways, such as "Maybe we can sit down together and look at solutions or find ways to make things more manageable?"

Replace feelings of guilt with self-compassion through journaling or mindfulness practices. Unhealthy guilt comes from unrealistic expectations or unreasonable expectations. Reflect on where your expectations of yourself are coming from. Are they realistic for your current energy capacity? For someone starting a new position?

Engage in self-compassion practices: journaling, therapy, or mindfulness can help you process feelings of guilt and replace them with gratitude and self-confidence.

Imposter Syndrome, Systemic Barriers, and Institutional Knowledge

Activity: Pride Affirmations

Reframe stereotypes and challenge their validity. Create affirmations celebrating the strengths derived from your background (e.g., "My unique experiences make me resilient and adaptable" or "The fact that I grew up poor allows me to think outside the box and do an amazing job creating streamlined budgets for my projects"). Repeating these daily can replace limiting beliefs with self-empowering ones.

Activity: Weekly Accomplishments File

Unfortunately, as first-gen college graduates, we tend to discount or even totally overlook our work accomplishments. Let's not have that be our MO! Take a quick minute at the end of every week to jot down what you've accomplished that you're proud of—whether it's taking on a challenging project, receiving positive feedback, or learning a new skill. Put it in a file and leave for the weekend. Look in that file when you experience self-doubt. Chances are that you will have forgotten some of the things you've done that demonstrate you're not a fraud and you bring value to your place of employment. You got this! Also, this practice reinforces your achievements and doubles as preparation for performance reviews. Also, tracking long-term accomplishments is crucial for career growth and professional development, especially when it comes to promotion.

Activity: Kaffeeklatsch Gathering

What can you do during those moments when you feel like you don't fit in at work and HR failed to give you the highly coveted *Handbook of Unwritten Work Rules* that everyone else got? And, quite honestly, your energy reserves needed to figure out what's going on are running empty! The answer isn't retreat and conserve that modicum of energy. Instead, it's regroup and channel your angst in a direction that serves and energizes you. Consider hosting a Kaffeeklatsch—a gathering that allows people from similar backgrounds or similar concerns to converse over coffee and share valuable information. Chances are excellent that you're not the only first-gen person where you work. Find allies within or outside your organization to create a space where you can share experiences you face as part of a specific identity. Let them know you want the focus to be on shared professional experiences—challenges, successes, and strategies for thriving. Be mindful that this activity is not intended to bad-mouth coworkers but instead to begin to build a supportive community helping combat isolation and systemic barriers. Your job is simply to put some energy into finding your people!

Chronic Stress and Burnout

Activity: Dimensions of Wellness Assessment

Identify two work challenges you experienced in the past two weeks that were draining and stressful. Using the eight dimensions of wellness graph below, choose two of the domains to focus on to decrease your stress level. Then identify an activity for each of those domains that you will engage in in the next two weeks to make that happen. Log your stress level today (0 = no stress, 10 = overwhelmed) and compare that value to your score two weeks from now. How'd you do? What worked and what didn't work? Commit to doing the activities that worked for the next two weeks.

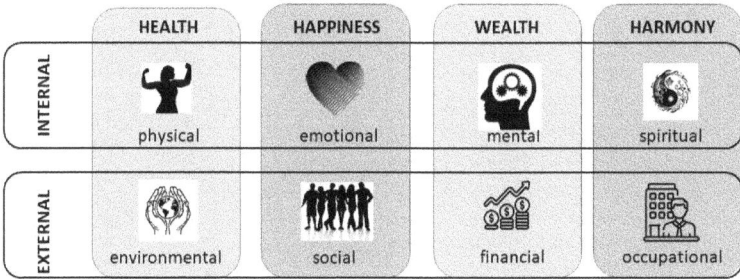

	HEALTH	HAPPINESS	WEALTH	HARMONY
INTERNAL	physical	emotional	mental	spiritual
EXTERNAL	environmental	social	financial	occupational

Activity: Eisenhower Matrix for Time-Management & Self-Care

Did you know that procrastination doesn't happen when we're struggling with time management but more so when we're struggling with self-care or managing our emotions when we feel anxious? Use the Eisenhower tool to prioritize tasks within a specific time frame such as weekly or daily. (The matrix was inspired by the time management philosophy of President Dwight D. Eisenhower and later popularized by Stephen Covey.) Make sure to include self-care tasks that are urgent and not urgent and schedule them as essentials. For instance, allocate time for exercise, rest, or spending time on hobbies that rejuvenate you. This prevents chronic stress from escalating into burnout.

	URGENT	NOT URGENT
IMPORTANT	**Do it** Things with clear deadlines and consequences for not taking immediate action. **Examples:** • Finishing a client project • Taking your sick dog to the vet	**Schedule it** Activities without a specific deadline that bring you closer to your goals. Easy to procrastinate on. **Examples:** • Professional Development • Networking
NOT IMPORTANT	**Delegate it** Things that need to be done but don't require your specific skills. Busy work. **Examples:** • Scheduling meetings • Meal prep	**Delete it** Distractions that make you feel worse afterward. Can by okay but only in moderation. **Examples:** • Social media • Eating junk food

Mental Health Challenges

Activity: Follow Your North Stars

Identify three values to guide you through the upcoming year. Write them down and put them somewhere they are easily accessible to you. Examples are balance, simplicity, positivity, focus, and patience. Not surprisingly, these words often apply to both your work life and your personal life. When traumatic memories and negative feelings like anxiety, self-doubt, and depression creep up for you, refer to your North Stars. Use them to get you back on track regarding your emotional well-being. Ask yourself, *Why am I feeling this way? What is going on for me that I'm not happy? How can I use my North Stars to redirect me so that I live a value-centered life that includes prioritizing my emotional well-being?* Importantly, you're likely going to change your words every year in response to your own growth and emerging insights about your emotional needs!

Activity: Personal Care Map or Care Compass

Create a help map with three sections: trusted people you can rely on (family, friends, mentors), professional resources (therapists, support groups), and self-help strategies (journaling, mindfulness). Keep this map easily accessible to use when challenges arise.

SELF-HELP MAP

CHAPTER 4

UTILIZING MENTORS

Personally, as a first-generation college student, I didn't have a mentor. Not as an undergraduate. Not while earning my graduate degrees. Not in the workforce. I don't recall even thinking about mentors, knowing anyone who had a mentor, or understanding the value of having a mentor. Not until about fifteen years ago. I'll explain more about that later.

Looking back, I can't help but wonder how my life may have been different if I had a mentor to guide and support me. My experience was from years back, but only 23 percent of more recent first-generation college graduates surveyed for this guidebook had mentors while in college and also while in the workforce. I can't help but wonder how the lives of those without mentors may have been different if they had a mentor to guide, support, and promote them to other professionals.

Why Have a Mentor?

Mentorship has been one of the most influential things in my life, and it's been one of the best decisions I have made. It's been a saving grace, as I've had mentors for many years.

—Shanicka S. Burdine

My role in my family growing up on the South side of Chicago was that person to set goals and plan for us. I was that person to resolve conflicts. I was that person to be that role model for my sisters and the rest of my family and to challenge limiting beliefs. In college, I needed guidance and advice about how college worked and someone I could talk to and feel supported.

—Nick M.

Do you know anyone who has gone through major life transitions without guidance and support of others? If you are fortunate to be one of the 26 percent of first-generation students in the United States who earn a college degree[iii], you know the challenge. Graduating from college and entering the professional workforce is considered one of the top five life transitions. It especially looms large to be the first in your family to chart your path through this new territory.

During the college-to-career transition, guidance and ac-countability for your work and life success are needed on a variety of matters, including emotional support, tactical support (such as résumé reviews), and strategic support (such as career planning). Perhaps you have a number of people in your life whom you trust and have the experience, wisdom, and your best interests in mind as they guide and support you in defining and reaching your goals, which is what mentors do. If so, great! Too often, however, as first-generation college graduates, our social and professional networks are not as robust as our continuing-generation college peers. We also don't have the financial resources to hire a professional career coach. That's where reaching out to potential mentors come in handy.

Who doesn't need emotional support? The quote above from Nick is not unusual. Many of us seek emotional support as we navigate challenges, rebuild our confidence, and stay motivated—even as younger siblings and others look to us as the first in our families to make this journey. Mentors are essential, as they encourage, empathize, reassure, and guide us. We know this instinctively and research which considers social validity, that is the perception of research participants that mentors made a positive difference, bears this out.

My mentor checked in on me informally several times the summer before starting my professional career and would listen to my goals and fears. She was there to offer encouragement and ease my worries about being in a challenging environment working alongside people that came from completely different socioeconomic backgrounds. Some words of advice that stuck with me were 'you'll never know what you can do if you don't try' and 'you wouldn't have this opportunity if you weren't ready and deserving of it.' This helped me start my career with a strong mindset.

—Beca C.

Who can't benefit from feedback before finalizing a résumé or cover letter? Who can't benefit from getting advice on how to negotiate a job offer? Did you know that mentors may be uniquely qualified to do this? Mentors provide this type of tactical support and more.

My mentor helped me with my résumé, *provided feedback, wrote recommendation letters, and helped me prepare for interviews.*

—Ivy Wilcher

And who doesn't have goals that can be more easily met from their mentor's insights on how to achieve them? Strategic and targeted support from mentors can help you make informed decisions, grow professionally, and effectively plan for your future success.

My mentor encouraged me to take on projects that supported my interests and challenged me to expand my skills.

—Talysha Rivera

Why Not?

If mentors can be so helpful, then why don't more of us first-generation college students have one? Like me, you may not have known or thought about it. Perhaps you don't understand what a mentor is and how you can benefit by having one. Perhaps you don't realize that mentors often find the role equally rewarding—as a way of giving back, as a way of learning about the mindset of the next-generation workforce, and as a way of understanding what is and is not working well for those entering the organization.

Many of us are used to fending for ourselves and tapping into the relationships we already have instead of branching out and developing new relationships. Whatever the reason is that you haven't had a mentor (e.g., time constraints, fear of judgment, cultural/social barriers, or worrying that it seems too transactional), now knowing how you can benefit, what's holding you back?

What if you had multiple mentors? Why not now?

How Do I Find a Mentor?

There is both formal and informal mentoring.

Formal mentoring through structured programs is often available within universities and nonprofit organizations as well as through employers and professional organizations. The goals of these formal programs may vary. For instance, university-based mentoring programs might have the goal of student retention for at-risk student groups. Employers who offer mentoring programs might have the goal of promoting employee professional development.

How do you find out if your university has a mentoring program? You can search on the university's website, ask your academic adviser, or check with any student groups or scholarship programs in which you're involved.

How do you know if your employer offers a mentoring program? You can ask during an interview what types of professional development opportunities exist or see if mentoring is mentioned as one of the opportunities. You can also check with the human resources department. With 98 percent of Fortune 500 companies[iv] providing employee mentoring programs, your chances of a workplace mentoring program are good. Even those of us who work for smaller organizations have options. You can find a mentor, but it might be through a nonprofit organization or a university alumni network rather than your employer.

How do you find out about nonprofit mentoring organizations? Oftentimes professional associations offer mentoring programs, such as the Society of Women Engineers and the American Nurses Association. In addition to professional associations, you can search online with broad keywords, such as "mentoring programs near me," or more specifically, such as "mentoring programs for college graduates," or even more granular, such as "mentoring programs for Black male college graduates."

I was initially assigned a mentor as a new hire. Eventually I decided to request mentors that were people I admired and wanted to learn from, and I did so by simply speaking up and simply asking them.

—First-gen alum

This first-gen alum shifted from formal mentoring in the workforce to informal mentoring. Informal mentoring is usually based on organically bred relationships between colleagues, friends, and family. Or it could be intentional, where you search for someone who you believe can provide guidance and other types of support you need to accomplish your goals. Perhaps this is someone you meet at a conference or someone you meet through your peer group or someone you seek out because you want to emulate their career path. Unlike formal mentoring programs that typically have a matching process and requirements for participating, informal mentoring is unstructured and is shaped by what *you* want it to be.

Fortunately, I've had dynamic, curious, and supportive teachers along my path who have naturally shifted into a mentorship role. They were invested, and are invested, in my continued development. For me, it happened quite naturally. And, because I am a curious person, I am happy to ask questions from those who have perspectives that can elevate my inner-standing.

—A. Raheim White

A's point is an important one. Genuine curiosity drives more meaningful conversations, an essential ingredient in mentoring relationships. It also draws out the mentor's experiences, lessons, and perspectives on topics that may not have surfaced otherwise. As the mentee, curiosity also leads to self-reflection, helping to explore your own goals, strengths, and areas of improvement more deeply.

> *As a first-generation college graduate, what I wish I knew when I first entered the professional workforce is to find peer mentors, not only management/leadership role mentors. A peer-to-peer mentor can be more approachable, available, and transparent with his or her experiences.*
>
> —Jarron F.

Jarron's experience is worth highlighting. By facilitating knowledge sharing, providing emotional support, and holding each other accountable, peer mentors play a critical role in helping employees thrive in their careers. They should not be overlooked.

> *Do not only seek out mentors who look like you.*
>
> —Jasmine W.

In my experience of facilitating mentoring partnerships over the past fifteen years, I would always ask the mentee if race and gender mattered to them in finding a mentor. Up until a few years ago, about 10 percent of students requested a mentor who shared the same race and/or gender. That changed, especially for Black women who wanted other Black women as their mentors. Having a mentor who looks like you can foster strong rapport, shared understanding, and inspiration, but it may also reduce your options if your interests are in a domain where there are few people like you. Also, it may reduce your exposure to diverse ways of thinking. Balancing a mentoring relationship with someone who shares your identity alongside mentors from different backgrounds can provide the most holistic and enriching development experience. That's Jasmine's point.

What's My Role in a Mentoring Relationship?

I just haven't had the best experience as far as mentorship. And I had to really sit down, self-reflect, and determine why... is it my lack of consistency? The lesson I learned and hope to teach others is when you enter a mentorship, it's on you to build that relationship and be consistent in keeping in touch with your mentor. Because nine times out of ten, you're working with someone who's busy, who's carving time out to support you and honestly, may not have the time to think of you or check in. It's on you to build and foster that relationship. I didn't always understand this and I still struggle today with being proactive. I'm a work in progress.

—J. M.

J. M. is right—it's on you to build and maintain a mentoring relationship. What do you need to know in order to do that?

First, consider if you're mentorable. Here are some questions to ask yourself:

- **Do you value your mentor's time?** The answer has to be yes; it's a rare commodity they are giving you.

  o Arrive early to your meetings.

  o Come prepared with your agenda for the meeting.

  o Actively engage with your mentor by leading the meeting rather than asking them to lead it. Own it!

  o Never leave them hanging; respond to emails or text messages within twenty-four hours.

Pretty basic, right? Surprisingly, when things go off track in a mentoring partnership, it's often because of these reasons.

- **Are you clear what you're looking for from a mentor?** What are the realistic reasons why you want a mentor (emotional support or tactical support that is immediate and actionable, or strategic support for longer-term planning)? Knowing the reasons can help you articulate your expectations and point you to a mentor who is more likely to be able to meet your needs.

- **Are you open to advice?** It's something you are seeking, but are you ready to receive their feedback? It's up to you whether you accept or reject their advice. But if you disagree, ask yourself why and make sure you're disagreeing for the right reasons instead of being defensive. Even with the best intentions, advice for one person might not work for another person based on their circumstances. No matter if you agree or disagree with their advice, make sure you express your gratitude. After all, they've put thought into the advice they gave to you.

- **Are you asking yourself periodically, *Am I a good mentee?*** Don't forget to reflect on your behaviors and whether you continue to value learning from your mentor during the mentoring partnership.

Second, understand your propensity to trust.

> *Trust is usually not given. It's simply earned, because many people have been let down in so many different ways and facets in their lives.*
>
> —Shanicka S. Burdine

Propensity to trust describes how likely it is that you will enter new relationships with a high level of trust. It often relies on past experiences, whether positive or negative. As Shanicka notes, many of us have been let down by others and, therefore, might start a mentoring relationship with a lower propensity to trust, meaning it will take more time to build trust. Do you know if you have a lower or higher propensity to trust?

Example of Propensity to Trust Questions.

How would you rate yourself on a scale of low (1) to high (5)?

1. I usually trust people unless they give me a reason not to trust them.
2. Trusting other people is not difficult for me.
3. I generally believe that others can be counted on to do what they say they will do.
4. I generally give people the benefit of the doubt when I first meet them.

Having this self-awareness is the baseline in working to build a trusting relationship with your mentor. You'll probably be looking for a combination of integrity, reliability, authenticity, empathy, competence, humility, respectfulness, and openness in your mentor's words and behaviors. These are trust-building traits. These qualities create an environment of mutual respect, reliability, and understanding that allows for deeper connections and stronger, more reliable relationships. Not only will you be looking for these traits in your mentor, but your mentor will be looking for these and other traits in you.

Building relationships requires moving at the speed of trust.

—Chelsa Moore

Chelsa's point reflects the understanding that trust is the key driver in relationships. Trust dictates how quickly you and your mentors can engage fully, share openly, and work toward meaningful goals. By aligning the mentoring relationship with the level of trust, both of you ensure a more authentic, comfortable, and ultimately productive dynamic.

Third, reflect on how you build and maintain friendships. What is similar and what is different with a mentoring relationship?

Sometimes it's easy to confuse relationships with friends with those you have with mentors. Both have a lot in common, such as emotional support and guidance, trust, and mutual respect. Both types of relationships can help us grow. There are also key differences, though: mentoring relationships are formal, they are limited in duration, they have clear boundaries, and they are designed with explicit mutual expectations. Mentoring is a volunteer service, and there is the utmost level of integrity that you expect from a mentor. While both mentors and friends provide emotional support, friends typically share equally whereas mentors focus on your goals.

Perhaps after you've accomplished the goals you are working on with your mentor, the relationship evolves into a friendship. I've seen this happen among my former students and their mentors. But it should not start out that way.

Here is a helpful hint: you are not the only one who benefits from a mentoring relationship. As noted earlier, mentors value the chance to learn from peers and from the next generation. Seeing the world through your eyes helps them in their developmental and leadership roles. When it goes well, there is two-way learning in a mentoring relationship. Also, many mentors were themselves first-generation students, and this is one of their ways of giving back.

What Are Some Supportive Alternatives to One-on-One Mentorship?

One-third of our survey respondents espoused the importance of having a mentor. They also pointed to alternative ways to garner support.

Finding Allies

Allies work with you in advancing a shared agenda. They can be collaborators, partners, supporters, colleagues, or others.

1. These are people you seek out within your organization who you can trust and who have your back.

2. The relationship is less about mentoring and more about working together to overcome barriers or achieve objectives.

3. Allies can provide encouragement, share resources, offer constructive feedback, and help you navigate challenges.

Learn the work culture quickly; figure out who you can turn to for assistance and who you can trust.

—K. Y.

But how do you identify and cultivate allies? One way is to observe them during meetings or in the lunch room. Pay attention to see if they share your values and goals when they respond to situations. Similarly, look for colleagues who others turn to for advice, support, or leadership, even if they aren't in formal leadership roles. Every workplace has these go-to individuals who may not be in positions of authority. Engage them in collaborative projects or offer help when needed. Consider asking them to meet for lunch or coffee so that you can learn more about them and, most importantly, help them to get to know you. Don't lurk in the shadows. Alliances are often built on shared experiences and support.

Sample Questions to Ask a Potential Ally

1. Tell me about what you do here at [Organization].

2. What about your work do you like and what would you like to change about your work?

3. I appreciate what you are doing with respect to [project]. How can I help?

4. I am encountering barriers with respect to [situation]. Can you help me to understand what I am encountering?

5. (If appropriate), your project sounds really interesting. If there's an opportunity, I'd like to help you with it

---

Utilizing Resources

This is when you can leverage services and networks available to you, such as ones through your college or university and your workplace.

> *Be resourceful...you don't have to be an island by yourself just because you're the first.*
>
> —Jasmine W.

While you're still in or even out of college, utilize the alumni network. How? Check out your college's website or alumni office for upcoming events such as reunions or professional networking events. Attending these in person or virtually to meet alumni in your field or geographic area is an excellent way to make meaningful connections. While in the workplace, get involved in employee resource groups (ERG), affinity groups, or other internal networks, if available. Attending meetings and events gives you the opportunity to meet like-minded people in a relaxed setting.

What if you earned a reputation as a valued contributor? Why not put yourself out there?

Building a Support Network

> *I really like where I'm at today. But yes, I would change a lot of things. I'd definitely reach out to more people in my network. I don't know why, I*

thought I was like laser focused on one thing, and no one else could understand. Clearly, there's a lot of people that have gone through the same thing as me, like corporate culture difficulties. I would have had someone sit down with me and really talk about it with someone who may have also had a similar experience in their first role . . . just so we could have bounced ideas and tried to understand what was happening.

—Noe Gill

Create your own board of directors—a diverse group of people you can go to who you can use as sounding boards to bounce things off of. This will be tremendously helpful throughout your professional career as you encounter work-related challenges or need input on an idea or project you are working on.

—Jasmine Colon

Find your support system outside of work.

—Justin W.

Think of building your support network as a DIY project. You're in charge of finding the people you need in your life to help you reach your goals. You're not relying on just one person because one person may not have all the knowledge, experience, skills, personal attributes, and networks that you need. When constructing corporate boards of directors, professionals set up a matrix with names across the top and categories as the rows. Then they make sure they have individuals who check the box on at least one of the rows. You can do the same thing!

How to begin? Identify people in your life who are positive, support your goals, challenge you to grow, and are thriving in their own career. Perhaps you want someone who is in your field or industry. Perhaps you want someone who is more seasoned but has a similar early-career story or comes from a similar socioeconomic status. Perhaps you only have one or two people now who meet your criteria. That's okay; over time you'll grow your network and find additional people who can offer the support you need. As with mentorability, it is also important to respect their time, know what you're looking for in each person, be open to advice, and periodically assess if you need to spend more or less time with those in your support network or your personal board of directors. Your circumstances will change, as will theirs.

I want to conclude by circling back to my own story of not having any mentors or being engaged in mentorship until about fifteen years ago. It was in 2007 that I met low-income, mostly first-generation college students at a large, land grant university who were part of a needs-based grants program (Illinois Promise). After hearing some of their stories and reflecting on my own undergraduate college experience, I couldn't help but wonder how they were going to survive on that large campus.

At the time I was working with a team to redevelop land for an intergenerational, multicultural, living learning community on campus. I was involved based on my expertise with and on behalf of older adults. With this background, I immediately wanted to bridge my experience working with older adults to support the Illinois Promise students. How did I do this? By initially creating an intergenerational mentoring program, followed by a peer mentoring program, so students could have a choice in selecting a mentor.

About one-third of all freshman Illinois Promise scholars per year (approximately 115 students) voluntarily chose a mentor. A number of those mentoring partnerships continued through graduation and to this day. I've witnessed the transformative power of mentoring relationships, and I've also seen mentoring relationships that never launched or faltered in the early stage. J. M.'s point is worth repeating—it's on you to build and foster that relationship.

What if you sought guidance from someone who has been where you want to go? Why not become a mentor yourself and inspire others to reach new heights?

CHAPTER 5

FINANCIAL ADVICE

If you're not in a social group where finances are part of the conversation, you just don't know what you don't know.

—Manuel Gomez

Have you ever thought about how little financial advice is shared among first-gen college grads and first-gen college students about to enter the workforce? I was surprised when I found out how rare it is. In a survey we conducted with early- to mid-career first-gen professionals, only 15 percent of women and just 3 percent of men offered financial advice to first-gen students about to enter the workforce. It sounds like Manuel was onto something.

Financial stress is a real thing. Many of us who are first-gen grads face serious financial pressures. We're juggling student loans, trying to support ourselves, and possibly carrying the expectation of helping out our families financially. And then there's the reality that those entry-level salaries don't always cover all our needs, adding to our already heightened level of anxiety.

> *The amount of money I earned was a challenge. It was only a part-time position and no benefits ($15/hour). Luckily, I still lived with my parents.*
>
> —Diego F.

Not everyone has the financial benefit of living with their parents after college, though. I know some former students who were couch surfing until they could afford to live on their own after graduation.

So here's the real question: Do you have enough money saved up after college to cover your first and last month's rent plus a security deposit? How are you going to move all your belongings to the city where you'll be working? Do you have money for essentials like a bed? Can you cover your basic monthly living expenses like rent, phone bills, utility bills, groceries, and transportation? And then there's the looming student loan payments. If you're invested in work-life balance, then a night out with friends every so often would be nice, wouldn't it? What if you lose your job? The stress of it all can be overwhelming. I get it. Planning ahead is key.

> *As first-gen recent college graduates, we usually come from less-privileged backgrounds without access to financial literacy tools. We are used to having little, and we know how to handle having little, how to stretch our money to meet*

all of our basic needs; but we are not used to having discretionary income that we could utilize efficiently to maximize future financial stability.

—Khanh Ngo

Khanh adds another perspective: Even if you know how to manage with less, maybe you don't necessarily know how to handle your discretionary income, which is the extra money you have in your checking account after you pay your basic living expenses.

Financial advice is so important at every stage of life. I asked about two dozen first-gen college grads and young professionals to share one piece of financial advice they'd give to someone just starting out. Their answers, along with some expert tips, are provided below. You may not have had enough straight talk on finances, so let me get real with you now.

Gain Financial Literacy

Learn as much as you can about personal finance as early as you can. The personal finance habits you start in your early 20s will stick with you. Your habits (not just financial) have compounding effects, so make sure they're good ones.

—Grace B.

For a first-gen grad, getting a handle on personal finance is a game changer. It's not just about budgeting (though that is important), it's also about understanding how money works so you can make smart decisions about your future. Since many of us didn't grow up learning about money at home, it's even more important to understand things like budgeting, saving, debt management, and investing.

College brings new opportunities, but it also brings financial challenges—like student loans. If you can learn about money early on, you'll avoid some common pitfalls like overspending, getting stuck in credit card debt, or not saving enough for your future.

I remember a recent grad who could get by using public transportation, but it wasn't convenient, especially when she needed to visit her mom. Her mentor suggested not buying a car, but she did anyway, using her savings to buy a used one. This left her with little emergency money. She ended up leaving her job before finding another one and had to rely on credit cards to pay her bills. This made her first year out of college more financially stressful than it might have been had she been more forward-thinking regarding her financial situation.

Becoming more financially literate will help you feel more confident making big decisions, like buying a house, planning for retirement, or building up an emergency fund. Having a personalized financial road map (and sticking to it!) is empowering because it puts you on the path to financial independence that is crucial, especially when you don't have a family safety net.

Here are six strategies experts recommend for building financial literacy.

1. **Practice mindful spending:** Do you really need it, or do you just want it? Even if you need it, are you getting the best price? Making thoughtful spending decisions and shopping smart can help you build good financial habits early on.

2. **Start with the basics:** Budgeting, saving, managing debt, and understanding credit is essential. These activities are your financial foundation. More information about these basics is included in this section of the guidebook.

3. **Take advantage of financial education tools:** Banks and financial institutions often offer free workshops or online courses. Check them out!

4. **Find a financial mentor (or a mentor who can provide financial advice):** Get advice from people who've been in your shoes. Hearing how someone else managed their loans or their first paychecks can be super helpful.

> **HR Pro Tip**
>
> Check your employer's employee assistance programs (EAP) and 401(k) vendor. These benefits sometimes include access to financial advisers and other financial services.

5. **Learn about student loan repayment:** Student loans are a big deal. Do you know about repayment plans, interest rates, and forgiveness

programs? Resources like StudentAid.gov or a loan adviser can help you understand your options.

6. **Start learning about investing:** You don't need a lot to start. Look into employer-sponsored retirement plans, like a 401(k), or use low-cost platforms like Vanguard, Fidelity, and Schwab. Check to see if you qualify to invest in a Roth IRA, which allows you to contribute after-tax income now so your money can grow tax-free and be withdrawn tax-free in retirement, maximizing long-term gains by starting early. Investing early helps your money grow over time.

Take it one step at a time. You don't have to learn everything at once—just start with mindful spending and the basics, then build from there.

Budgeting

Everyone can create a budget—it's one of the most practical and essential tools for anyone aiming to take control of their finances.

—Bianca Flowers

Why is budgeting so important? It gives you control over your money. Without one, it's way too easy to lose track of where your money's going.

Ever heard of the 50/30/20 rule? Experts usually recommend putting 50 percent of your budget toward needs (rent, utilities, groceries, transportation), 30 percent toward wants (entertainment, fun stuff), and 20 percent toward savings.

And if you're a 1099 contractor, you'll be responsible for paying quarterly federal, state, and city taxes. How much you pay depends on your federal tax bracket (you can find this online at irs.gov). Taxes fit in the need category.

Think of your budget like a road map. When you know exactly where you stand financially, you can make better decisions about spending or cutting back. Plus, it helps you feel more prepared when those unexpected expenses pop up. And they *will* pop up!

There are some great free resources out there, like Mint and EveryDollar, that can help you get started with budgeting. Remember, how you spend your money reflects your values!

Emergency Savings

As soon as possible, start an emergency fund savings account. Life after college is very vulnerable and can take so many unexpected turns. You never know when you will need to rely on your emergency funds. It is better to be ready than need to get ready.

—Gisel Ureña

Having an emergency fund is like having a safety net. Gisel's right—life can get unpredictable. Imagine if your car breaks down, your cat needs dental surgery, or you get hit with an unexpected medical bill. Without some savings set aside, things like that can really mess up your finances. An emergency fund gives you a cushion to handle those surprises without having to max out your credit cards, take out a loan, or ask someone else for help.

It's all about protecting yourself from falling into debt and giving you peace of mind, knowing you've got some money tucked away for life's curveballs. It also helps you stay on track with your other goals, like saving for a house or building up retirement savings.

Experts usually recommend saving three to six months' worth of living expenses in an emergency fund. It sounds like a lot, but here's the key: figure out how much you spend on essentials each month—like rent, groceries, and bills—then aim to save enough to cover at least three months' worth of those costs, and ideally up to six.

Now how much you save depends on your situation. If you've got a stable job and you're single, three months might be enough. But if you have kids or family responsibilities, or you're in an industry where layoffs are common, you might want to shoot for six months or more.

Don't worry if saving that much feels overwhelming at first—it's okay to start small. Building an emergency fund takes time, and even having a few hundred dollars set aside can make a difference when something minor pops up. The important thing is to just start.

Savings

Start saving early and save as much as you can.

—Khanh Ngo

On top of having an emergency fund, saving regularly is super important, especially for first-generation college grads. It's about giving yourself more financial security and flexibility as you begin your career. Try to get into the habit of setting aside money consistently—ideally putting it in a high-yield savings account or a money market account.

Remember the 50/30/20 rule? That 20 percent part of your budget can go toward both your emergency fund and regular savings. But if 20 percent seems like too much right now, don't stress—it's okay to start smaller. The goal is to build the habit, even if you're only saving 10 percent of your income at first. Little by little, you'll get there.

Debt Management

I'm sure you're wondering how to balance saving with paying off student loans or credit card debt. Experts recommend focusing on high-interest debt first, setting up a basic emergency fund, and then creating a plan to save while paying off debt over time.

Start by figuring out what kind of debt you have. High-interest debt, like credit cards, should be your priority because interest can add up fast. The interest on this kind of debt is usually way higher than any return you'd get from a savings account. So pay on time and pay off the statement balance. Do not only pay the minimum. Also, do not use credit cards to spend on wants you cannot pay off immediately. This can get you in trouble with debt.

When it comes to budgeting, debt repayment falls under the needs category—the 50 percent part of your budget. Depending on how much debt you have and what other expenses you're dealing with, you might need to adjust those percentages for a while.

While experts recommend having three to six months' worth of expenses in your emergency fund, if you're balancing debt, it's okay to start small. A mini emergency fund of $500 to $1,000 can protect you from unexpected expenses and stop you from relying on credit cards for emergencies, which could make your debt worse.

Once you've got a basic emergency fund in place, you can focus more on paying off your debt while still saving for the future. It helps to set clear goals both short-term (like saving for a trip, a wedding, or a new gadget) and long-term (like buying a house or retiring). Having these goals can keep you motivated to save, even while paying down debt.

One great tip is to set up automatic transfers to your savings account. That way you're saving consistently without even having to think about it.

Credit

> *Healthy debt will make you lendable in the eyes of creditors. Take out two credit cards, one you'll seldom use and another you'll use for bills. Never miss a payment, and after a year you should have enough credit to purchase a car, furniture, condo, etc. Bonus points if the credit card offers points or statement credits.*
>
> —Tony V.

Building good credit is crucial, especially for young professionals. It affects everything from getting a car loan to renting an apartment. Tony's advice is solid—use credit wisely and always pay on time. Ideally, keep your credit card balances at zero, or at least very low, using less than 30 percent of your available credit.

Your credit score is a big deal for lenders. It ranges from 300 to 850, and the higher your score, the more creditworthy you look to lenders. Being creditworthy not only allows you to get loans, but it can also get you lower interest rates on some types of loans. To improve your credit, make payments on time, keep your balances low, and have a mix of credit types (like credit cards, student loans, or auto loans). You should also check your credit report regularly to make sure everything's accurate. You can get a free report annually from each of the three major credit bureaus: Experian, TransUnion, and Equifax.

If you don't have any credit, you can look for secured cards—where you put down a small deposit—to start building. Once you've got some credit history, you can look into cashback cards to get a little something back on what you spend.

Investing

Always pay yourself first. You've done the work and you deserve to be paid. In paying yourself, let your money make money. It's never too early to invest. Break the cycle and do something different (prosperous) to set up future generations.

—Shanicka S. Burdine

At some point, you'll want to start investing—letting your money make money. Investing involves risk (you could lose part or all of the money you invest). You need to understand your tolerance for risk before investing. It might feel a little overwhelming at first, especially if no one in your family has really talked about investing before, but it's one of the most powerful ways to build wealth over time.

Here's some advice to get started:

1. **Start early, even if it's small.** The earlier you invest the more time your money has to grow. You don't need a lot to begin—just start with what you can afford.

2. **Educate yourself.** Learn the basics of investing. There are books, podcasts, and online courses that break it down in simple terms. A couple of podcasts that former students recommend are *Wealth Redefined* and *The Dave Ramsey Show.*

3. **Set clear goals.** Are you saving for a trip? A house? Your retirement? Having clear goals helps you stay focused.

4. **Diversify your investments.** Don't put all your money in one type of investment. Spreading it out across stocks, bonds, real estate, and so on can reduce risk. If one investment doesn't perform well, others might balance it out.

5. **Consider retirement accounts.** If your employer offers a 401(k) or matching contributions, take advantage of it. And look into IRAs—especially Roth IRAs if you financially qualify—for retirement savings.

6. **Stick to your plan.** Don't try to time the market. Focus on long-term growth and stick with your strategy even when the market gets shaky.

7. **Review and adjust regularly.** Check your investments at least annually to ensure they align with your goals. You might need to adjust your portfolio as your life circumstances change, like getting a new job, buying a home, or starting a family.

8. **Seek professional advice if needed.** If you feel overwhelmed, consider talking to a financial adviser. They can help you develop a personalized investment strategy based on your goals and risk tolerance. Make sure you understand the costs involved. That is, how does the adviser make money when they work with you?

Setting Financial Boundaries

You cannot take care of everyone. Many first-gen college students may be viewed as or feel as if they are the most stable person in their family when it comes to finances and other socioeconomics factors. With that said, they may sign up to take on responsibilities that they are not quite ready for. In this current global landscape graduating from college is typically the first step in your professional and personal journey. I strongly advise first generation students to ensure that their glass is running over before they pour into anyone else's cup.

—Tatiana Smith-Blakely

Tatiana nailed it. As first-gen grads, we often feel like we're the most stable person in our family, but that doesn't mean we can take on responsibilities we aren't ready for. It's easy to get caught up in helping everyone, but remember—you have to take care of yourself first.

Setting financial boundaries with loved ones can be tough, but it's necessary. If someone's counting on you financially, here's a conversation starter (a longer version using the DEAR MAN approach is in chapter 3):

"I've been thinking about how much we've always supported each other. I want to talk about something important— finances. As you know, I'm just starting out and working hard to build my financial stability. Right now, I can't help you financially until I get more financial stability, but I'd love to brainstorm other ways I can be supportive."

This approach is calm, respectful, and empathetic. Setting boundaries doesn't mean you don't care—it just means you're protecting your own financial well-being.

If you are ready to help family members, one option to consider is budgeting for family. Whatever percent of your budget you set aside for your family will come from another part of your budget (such as your wants).

Once you know better, you begin to consider what doing better looks like.

—Shanika S. Burdine

Once you understand how money works—whether it's budgeting, savings, managing debt, or investing—you start thinking differently about your choices. Maybe earlier in your life you didn't think twice about living paycheck to paycheck, but now that you know better, you start planning for an emergency fund or paying off debt faster.

It's about progress, not perfection—doing better with what you know now.

What if you took this advice to create lasting financial stability? Why not take steps today and build over time?

CHAPTER 6

DEVELOPING AS A PROFESSIONAL

It was hard adjusting to being "in charge" of a program area, where I am expected to lead, having only been in jobs where I was in more supportive positions.

—Victoria L.

Time management was the biggest challenge. Spending too much time on one task would take time away from the next. A domino effect you can't afford in the professional world.

—Rachel Lloyd

I struggled with emotional intelligence and didn't know how to receive feedback. I was also shy and intimidated to ask for help. I had to learn through failing.

—Chelsa Moore

One thing I wish I would have known was how to be a better networker. I still struggle with networking today. Strong networking can lead to mentors and job leads. It's very important and necessary in the corporate world.

—J. M.

Based on these selected quotes, what do you think is the biggest challenge college grads face when they start working? Hint: it's not the same for women and men. (I'll get to possible explanations for that in a minute.)

A related question: According to the results of our survey, what is the most frequent type of advice first-gen college alums give to other first-gens as they enter the professional workforce? Hint: the type of advice is the same for men and women.

The answers to both questions involve professional skills, which are the focus of this chapter.

According to this survey, the top challenge first-gens faced when entering the professional workforce was developing professional skills (such as building soft or interpersonal and technical skills), continuous learning (e.g., earning online certifications), and networking. For men, the number one challenge was a very different set of professional skills—figuring out how to navigate corporate culture, which we'll dive into in the next chapter.

Professional development is very important for young professionals in general. It is one of the top attributes new college grads say is important in a job (along with job security, friendly coworkers, and a good benefits package).

So what do you look for in your job search process so that you will know if you're entering a culture that will support professional development? Assuming professional development is also important to you, here are some things to consider asking about before making a decision to accept a position:

1. **What is your budget for professional development?** This can include money for such things as conference travel, tuition to take a class relevant to your job, and books that would also improve your job knowledge and productivity.

2. **Are there LinkedIn offerings or in-house courses available?** Perhaps the company has a LinkedIn Learning benefit or has developed their own learning materials where you can acquire new knowledge and skills at your own pace.

3. **How do new employees get integrated into their roles and the organization?** Perhaps there's one-on-one coaching or an informal mentoring program.

4. **Is there a career path for the role in which you're being hired?** Career paths indicate that there are opportunities for learning new skills, gaining experience, and moving into more advanced roles.

5. **How long do employees typically remain in the same role?** If employees are in the same role for a long time, this could be a red flag and indicate a lack of professional development opportunities.

6. **Can you take time off for mental health reasons?** If so, this signals the company's investment in long-term professional success by ultimately helping individuals perform better and preventing burnout. If the organization is not receptive to this question, this suggests that employee wellness is not one of their core values.

HR Pro Tip

Don't be afraid to ask how they support work-life balance for their employees. This can help you gain insight into their approach to mental health in the workplace.

Do you know what skills you want to develop professionally? If so, this points to self-awareness, which is an essential skill to have in and of itself. Self-awareness includes knowing your career goals. What kinds of roles and responsibilities do you want to develop? What skills are listed in those types of job descriptions? Without knowing the answers to these two questions, you will not have clarity on the skills necessary to excel in your job. Self-awareness also includes honestly assessing your strengths and areas for improvement in your current role.

What if you don't yet know your career goals but still want to develop more skills? How do you figure out which skills to prioritize? First, observe others. What skills do they possess that you want to emulate? Perhaps it's a soft skill like leading a team or perhaps it's a technical skill like analyzing data and opportunities to present the results to executives at the organization. Second, request and accept feedback. It's more than okay to ask your manager for feedback, as it shows initiative and a desire to improve. In soliciting and accepting feedback, just remember to keep a positive tone, be humble, and sincerely express a willingness to learn so you can continue to grow professionally. Here's an example of what you could say:

"Hi [Manager's Name], I'd really appreciate your feedback on my recent presentation. Specifically, I'd like to know if there are any areas where I could improve, especially on what I presented and on my delivery. I find regular feedback really helpful for my growth. I'd also like to set up a monthly check-in to ensure I'm meeting or exceeding your expectations. Would that be possible?"

After you receive the feedback, simply summarizing the key points shows that you heard the feedback given and will also help you remember when you need to do your next presentation. For example, you could say:

"Thanks so much, [Manager's Name]. That's really helpful feedback. Next time I'll remember to expand the number of slides I use so there isn't too much content on each. I'll also remember to look more at the audience and less at my slides."

The third way to figure out what professional skills you might need is by completing one or more self-assessments. Two well-known assessments are the Myers-Briggs Type Indicator (MBTI) and DiSC assessment. Isabel Myers and her mother, Cook Briggs, developed the initial version of the MBTI; DiSC is an acronym that stands for the four main personality profiles described in the DiSC model: (D)ominance, (i)nfluence, (S)teadiness, and (C)onscientiousness. Both are behavioral assessment tools designed to improve job performance by categorizing individuals into personality traits. By completing one or both of these assessments, you might learn what soft skills (how you interact with others and solve problems) are needed in order to work better with coworkers who have different personality traits than you do. There's also CliftonStrengths, which is an online assessment tool helping to identify your strengths. My former students were assigned to take this assessment as part of a university introductory course and found it helpful in giving them words to describe their strengths.

So why did more women compared to men list professional development skills (soft and technical skills, networking, and continuous learning) as the major challenge for them when they entered the professional workplace? While it's hard to know for sure, our focus group participants expressed these potential explanations: (1) history shows women have not had the same professional advantages as men (e.g., men have traditionally been promoted to leadership roles more frequently than women, partly due to deeply established networks, gender-driven stereotypes about leadership qualities, and biases in hiring and promotion practices), (2) women are more likely to question their abilities and as a result they seek knowledge and guidance from others about their abilities, and (3) as first-gen alums, most things felt new during the first job and perhaps women just wanted to get better at what they had to do (e.g., they may be more likely to take advantage of employer-sponsored training).

Whatever the reasons for the gender differences, here's some advice from both women and men first-gen young professionals for developing professional skills.

Goal Setting

Set achievable goals: daily, monthly, and yearly. Being able to look back on accomplishments is always so encouraging and builds self-worth and identity, which then translates into your confidence at work.

—Tiffany Remington

Those of us who set goals tend to be motivated by progress and a sense of purpose. As Tiffany said, accomplishing your goals also helps you with building confidence. Knowing you've done something before is growing proof that you'll be able to do it again and then again, with more self-assurance and perhaps with improvement as time progresses. This is how we develop.

We're not all excellent at everything at once! We need to give ourselves grace and keep at it. Experiencing proof of accomplishment (such as obtaining certifications, professional acknowledgments, etc.) is especially important for those of us with impostor syndrome, that feeling of self-doubt and personal incompetence despite our education, experience, and accomplishments we discussed in chapter 3. Imposter syndrome is typically experienced by women more so than men and by first-gen students more than continuing-gen students. Imposter syndrome can be a significant career development barrier.

Setting goals for your career also gives you a road map for the types of professional skills you need to develop along the way. If you're working at a large organization with career pathways that meet your goals, you'll have the road map laid out for you. If you're in a smaller organization or don't see yourself working for an organization for more than a couple of years, you need to design your own personal development road map based on your career goals.

It helps to make SMART professional development goals. SMART goals are covered in chapter 7.

Networking

I went about my professional life like my personal life...find the smartest person in the room. You should never be the smartest person in the room. That's for sure. Talk to them, pick their brains. Get from them what you need, because that's what it was at home growing up. I'm gonna get as much of my dad as I can before I know that he either has to go to work or he has to decompress, or has to be a father to my other siblings. Same thing with my mom. Let me get as much of this love, as much of this comfort as I can get because I know that's all I'm gonna get, and if I don't seek it out when I need it, it might not happen organically.

—Tony V.

Does networking feel like a dirty word to you? It probably doesn't feel that way to Tony even though it is often viewed as transactional and not authentic. If it does feel like a dirty word, reframe it as a crucial way of creating connections with mutual support instead of viewing it as self-serving. You certainly have something to share with others. Shifting your mindset from *What can I get out of this?* to *How can I create value for others?* will make networking feel much more authentic and positive.

I learned from my research during the Great Recession of 2007–2009 with continuing-gen college grads who were ten years out from completing their college degree that they relied on their networks much more frequently than first-gen college grads (also ten years out) in securing their first positions post college. However, in subsequent positions, first-gen alums caught up to the continuing-gen alums in utilizing their networks for career advancement. What do I take away from this finding? Personal networks are important for career opportunities for everyone; first-gen alums were just a little slower to discover how important it is to apply this lesson in their own lives.

And it's an important lesson to learn. As already noted, estimates range from 70 percent to 80 percent for jobs that are filled through personal connections or internal recommendations and are not advertised publicly.

A significant challenge we first-generation college students face is starting with less social capital, or professional connections, since we're charting new territory. We can't rely on our parents to introduce us to their professional colleagues for internships or jobs or to make other professional connections. Just like learning how to navigate and succeed in college as the first from our families, we need to learn how to build meaningful connections for our future professional selves.

Where to start? Take inventory. Who are you connected to? That is, who in your immediate and surrounding circles might be helpful to you? How strong are these relationships and how are they mutually beneficial? What's missing from your connections? Do you need to know more people in a certain discipline, in a certain industry, in a certain company? Someone perhaps who has a skill set you are aspiring to build? What's your plan for building the connections you need to get from where you're at now to where you want to go? These are important questions to ask yourself as you take inventory of your network in relation to your future career goals. Here's a template of an eco-map for you to get started in taking your own personal inventory. Create a current eco-map and a future eco-map with how you want your network to look a year from now and your plan for getting there.

Network – Eco-Mapping Template

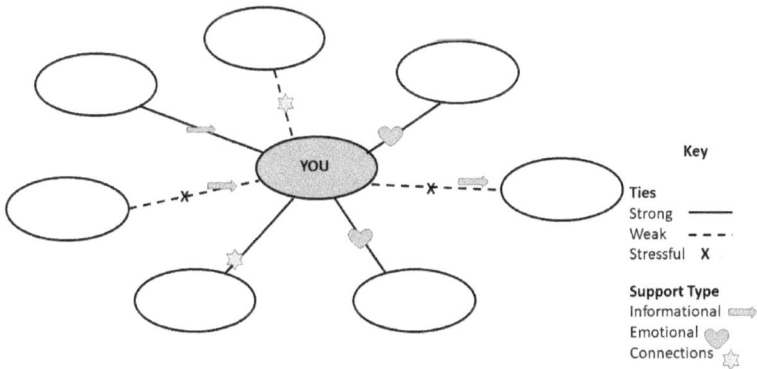

Even with reframing "networking" to "creating connections" so you're more comfortable, you might not know how to do it. Here are some tips for in-person and virtual networking:

In-Person Networking

This can be at professional conferences, alumni or charity events, social clubs, and even at a coffee shop or dinner party!

1. **Start small.** At a networking event, having a few meaningful conversations matters more than the number of business cards you get at the end of the event or the number of people you connect with via LinkedIn. This also means paying attention to the person you're talking with and not worrying about who you should be talking to next.

2. **Don't try to enter into a conversation with two people.** Two people conversing are most likely engrossed in their own conversation and less likely to welcome you in their conversation. Rather, find one person or a group of three or more to join. Smile, catch someone's eye, and introduce yourself.

3. **Prepare a conversation starter with a question.** One example is "What brought you to this event?"

4. **Create and deliver your elevator pitch.** This is a brief introduction (thirty to forty-five seconds) about yourself (including what you do/your passions and in some circumstances, like a job

fair, what you want). If the concept of an elevator pitch is new to you, you can find lots of examples by doing a quick web search. An elevator pitch is also described in chapter 1.

5. **Be a good listener.** Most people appreciate it when others are interested in what they have to say. How do you demonstrate that you're a good listener? One way is to simply restate a key point the person made that you appreciate, ask questions, share reflections, and provide advice or feedback.

6. **Be mindful of your body language.** Are you looking at them? Are you nodding and engaged? This body language also shows you are listening. How would you feel if you were talking to someone whose eyes kept gazing at others who walked by or who periodically checked their watch or phone? Don't be that person!

7. **Find mutual connections and interests.** Whether it's shared people you know, what you do for a living, or how you spend your free time, finding common ground will make the conversation seem more natural.

8. **Have an exit strategy.** Even if your goal is talking to two or three people over the course of an hour, think through what you're going to say to move on instead of just walking away. Here's one example: "It's been great chatting with you.

I'll connect with you on LinkedIn in the next couple of days." (Of course, you then need to follow through on this promise.)

9. **Follow up after the event.** If you sincerely want to keep in touch with people you met at an event, send them an email or connect with them on LinkedIn. Make reference to something specific in your earlier conversation. That's the easy part. What takes more time and thought is building the relationship so it's meaningful beyond the event in which you met.

Virtual Networking

Virtual networking may feel more comfortable to some people, but there are also challenges. It usually takes place over platforms like LinkedIn and Zoom. Some of the tips previously mentioned can apply to virtual networking events, such as conferences and webinars, but here are a few other tips:

1. **Turn on your video.** This makes interactions more personal. Make sure the light is in front and pointed at you (not behind you) so others can see your face. Make sure your background is simple and not offensive.

2. **Ask questions / share your insights.** Start by commenting in the chat if you're nervous about speaking up on video.

3. **Connect via LinkedIn.** Invite everyone who's attending to connect with you via LinkedIn. Add your link to the chat box, and chances are good that someone will reach out to you.

How about connecting to others online when it's not a virtual networking event? Here are some additional tips that you can use in this circumstance:

1. **Use direct messaging thoughtfully.** Your direct message should be concise and include how you found them and why you want to connect. Ask for a brief (ten-minute) meeting or virtual chat as appropriate.

2. **Leverage LinkedIn.** Personalize connection requests by referencing something specific, like an article they wrote or posted. Once connected, engage with their content by liking, commenting, or sharing posts, which can create a natural transition into a conversation. Also, join alumni or professional groups related to your field.

3. **Use email thoughtfully.** If you aren't using social media for direct messaging, email is also a great way to make connections. When crafting an email, take the time to personalize it and be

sure to reference common interests or something the recipient has done that inspires you. If
appropriate, ask for a brief video chat or phone
meeting.

Think about how often you connect with others in your
network and the quality of those interactions. Whatever
the frequency and the nature of those interactions, does
it feel sufficiently comfortable when reaching out to them
if you haven't spoken in a year? If not, how do you keep
those connections warm? Having worked with hundreds
of first-gen students over the past fifteen years, here are
some tips that have been used by them to keep in contact
with me and that I appreciate:

1. **Periodically check in.** Every three to six months,
   send a text or email to say hi, let them know that
   you're thinking of them, and ask, "How are you
   doing?" Who doesn't like to be thought about?
   Perhaps the timing of your periodic check-ins
   coincides with an upcoming event or another
   occasion that is meaningful in your relationship.
   If you have something to update them on in your
   life (a new job, a new baby, or a new dog), use
   these check-ins as an opportunity to do so.

2. **End-of-year greeting.** Sending a quick holiday
   or year-end greeting through text, email, or snail
   mail is a natural way to reach out. Something as
   simple as wishing them a happy holiday season
   and staying in touch in the New Year works well.

3. **Offer congratulations.** If there is someone in your network who has done something (won an award, got married, published an article, accepted a new job offer, etc.), send them a note of congratulations. It reinforces your support for them. And remember, this fits with reframing networking as building relationships and offering mutual support.

4. **Show gratitude.** Our achievements are not only based on our own efforts. We have people in our lives who have offered support in various ways. When your achievements are based on their support, let them know this through a note of gratitude.

Even now knowing all of these networking tips for building and maintaining your network and reframing it so you're more comfortable, you may still remain hesitant to attend an event or reach out to someone you want to know and learn from. Remember "what if" and "why not?" How's it going to happen unless you take action? Visualize all the good that can result.

What's the worst that can happen from networking? Why not now?

Skill Development

Invest in yourself. Take professional development classes, earn certifications, stay current in your field.

—Ivy Wilcher

One thing we can count on is a changing world. It doesn't stay stagnant so we shouldn't either. Because we live in a competitive marketplace, we need to demonstrate that we are "worthy" in order beat out the competition to get hired. We need to meet or exceed expectations in our current position to stay employed. And we need to build new skills for increased and varied responsibilities in our future roles. Some of these skills we'll learn on the job; the other skills we'll need to develop outside of our working hours.

> **HR Pro Tip**
>
> *Don't forget to tap into your employee benefits to support your professional development, whether on or off the clock.*

You should know what skills are required based on your job description. These are the skills you should first focus on improving. Having self-awareness and requesting feedback from your supervisor will help assess what gaps in your required skill set you need to close.

How about other skills beyond your job description? In 2024, the skill sets most employers were seeking in job candidates are problem-solving and teamwork skills[v]. The other top skills are written and verbal communication skills, analytical/quantitative skills, and technical skills. Personal attributes that matter to employers are a strong work ethic and adaptability and flexibility.

How do you fare with these skills? Perhaps you began developing these skills and attributes through class assignments, extracurricular activities, experiential learning, and internships or positions you've already held. That's great! But it doesn't mean you've mastered the skill set.

Think about what it takes to master a skill set. Can you perform the skill at a high level consistently without much thought or effort in different circumstances? Have you received accolades from others about how you performed the skill? While mastery of a skill is subjective, more likely than not there is always room for improvement. So work on developing the skills that matter in your current position, skills that matter to employers in general, and skills you anticipate needing based on your career goals. Internalize sports announcer Vin Scully's quote, "Good is not good when better is expected."

Continuous Learning

Don't be afraid to ask questions if you don't understand something, if something's not working.

—Brian F.

What do you do when you don't know something? Do you do your own research and only ask someone when you can't find the answer? If you don't ask questions, think about what's holding you back. Could it be because you're afraid you should already know the answer? Could it be you think you should find the answer on your own and not take someone else's time by asking? Whatever the reason, many first-gen alums who responded to our survey, like Brian, advised that it is important to ask questions in your professional role.

Be curious. Be a learner.

—Chelsa Moore

How about beyond your professional role? Do you typically ask a lot of questions? If so, it probably means you're curious, which is a good thing. It shows you're interested, and you want to learn.

Asking questions is just one way to continuously learn. Other ways you can be a lifelong learner include attending lectures; listening to podcasts; reading newspapers, magazines, and blogs; enrolling in classes; attending webinars; participating in opportunities found through your professional associations; engaging in conversations with a range of people, including strangers; traveling; and more. Information and opportunities are all around us to absorb, critically analyze, experience, and act upon. While continuous learning is related to skill development, it's broader than that. It's self-driven. It's a lifelong process of gaining knowledge related and unrelated to our work. It will make us more interesting and informed and lead to a fuller life. If you think about people you know who are continuously learning, wouldn't you agree? Continuous learning is both personal and professional development and is also highly advised by first-gen alums. Be curious!

What if you consistently invested in developing your skills and relationships? Why not take the initiative to grow, lead, and inspire others along the way?

CHAPTER 7

NAVIGATING AND ADVANCING YOUR CAREER

Understanding the norms and expected behaviors of the office environment, especially with coworkers who are much older than myself, was a major challenge.

—Ricardo P.L.

Many of the experiences that I encountered in the workplace weren't taught in a textbook. Learning how to navigate as a professional, fresh out of college and in a new environment away from my family support system, was a challenge during the first year of employment.

—Jasmine W.

Workplace Culture

Before you can advance your career, you need to navigate your way through your first position. Understanding workplace culture early on has a lot to do with how you do in that first position. This was the most frequently cited challenge reported by first-gen male alums in our survey. (It was cited, but it was not the top challenge reported by women; I'll present some possible explanations for this in a moment.) Ricardo's sentiments about learning the norms and expected behaviors were echoed by many others. As Jasmine says, how someone does this isn't usually taught in a textbook.

I recall a conversation I had with one of my former first-gen male students after he'd worked at one of the best consulting firms in the world for less than a year. He was so excited to receive the offer (his only offer after graduation) and said he could now "eat three meals a day" on his salary, an amount he never dreamed he would ever make. However, he said working at the consulting firm was "like watching a basketball game without knowing any of the rules." Though he had a mentor and asked lots of questions, the workplace culture was foreign (he lacked what is described in chapter 3 as institutional knowledge) and it was not relatable to him. He resigned before completing his first year at the firm.

So what do you do? How do you read between the lines? How do you understand the norms and workplace culture and determine if it's a place where you can grow with the organization? When do you call it quits? Here are some tips for understanding workplace culture:

1. **Observe communications.** How do people interact in meetings and in casual conversations? How would you describe the tone—for example, is it more competitive or collaborative? Is the tone consistent among different employees and between different levels of management? Are emails answered after hours? Does the workplace emphasize teamwork by using words like *we* and *us*, or are individual achievements more of the focus?

2. **Observe behaviors.** Identifying patterns helps reveal behavioral norms. Do people arrive early, stay late, lunch together, celebrate personal milestones?

3. **Workspace layouts.** Are there open floor plans, which encourage collaboration and transparency? Are there private offices, which may signal a more hierarchical and formal workplace?

4. **Take cues from leadership behavior.** Do leaders encourage questions and new ideas, or do they expect more compliance? This can signal a culture that leans either toward innovation or stability. Leaders' actions signal acceptable norms and boundaries for others.

5. **Note what is not said.** Tune your ears for unstated assumptions. Do managers assume people need to be monitored in their work or that people need to be supported? Is it okay to take risks, or do people pay a price if they do and it doesn't go as planned? If you figure out the unstated assumptions that are driving behavior, you can predict how things will go in meetings and on projects.

6. **What are the stated policies and procedures?** Do the policies signal appreciation for work-life balance? How is vacation time and personal leave time handled? Is there support for professional development? Even if the policies signal support for work-life balance, do people value and utilize these policies?

Based on what you observe in your workplace, are you able to adapt your approach? Cultures vary widely in what they expect from employees. Being able to adjust your behavior and communication style to align with these norms is a powerful skill. However, based on what you observe and learn, the culture might reflect a difference in values that are personally unacceptable. Only you can weigh the pros and cons and make a decision to learn and grow or call it quits with an organization.

Identifying the deeply embedded assumptions in a culture is not easy. They are not always stated explicitly, but show up as unstated "rules of the game." There are, nonetheless, rules that need to be understood and followed sufficiently to be effective in your work. Where you break from the rules, it should be on purpose, not by accident. For example, if there is an unstated rule that everyone works past five p.m. and you have plans that involve leaving at five, that's okay, but you may want to let key people know that your work is up-to-date and you're leaving for an appointment, meeting, or something else. This communication strategy signals that you understand the norms, but this day is an exception. Of course, if you are someone who resents having to work late as a norm, then this organization may not be a good fit for you.

Why might men, but not women, report navigating workplace culture as the number one challenge? In fact, only 11 percent of women compared to 32 percent of men in our survey reported workplace culture as a challenge. Some possible explanations to this question that emerged from our focus group include the following: (1) women may have more experience navigating different cultures, especially living in a male-dominated society; (2) men may be more likely to ask for forgiveness, whereas women may be more likely to ask for permission; and (3) women may perceive culture as all-encompassing in society and, as such, it's not a top priority in a particular workplace. They may choose to focus their energies on aspects of their job they have more control over, such as completing a concrete work assignment.

Communication: Feedback

In addition to workplace culture, how you communicate and conduct yourself in the workplace can help or hurt your opportunities for advancement. Ultimately, your soft skills are what's going to help you progress. Of course, it can take hard work to develop excellent soft skills.

Feedback—both giving and receiving—are key communication skills.

Learn to accept constructive criticism/feedback.

—Diego F.

Imagine you're in your first professional position after college, and you've done a good job at observing and learning about workplace culture. You've just turned in your first report, and your supervisor wants to give you feedback. How do you feel? Are you excited, apprehensive, afraid, or do you have another dominating emotion?

Feedback is a gift. All too often in life, we don't get it. Why? Perhaps people are afraid of the impact it will have on your relationship with them or perhaps they aren't skilled at giving feedback. Whatever the reason, feedback is a gift that can help you develop. And who doesn't want to grow and further develop professionally? So with that lens, here's an example of how you can openly receive feedback.

Supervisor: *"I've noticed how dedicated you've been about writing the report and meeting deadlines. Overall, I like what you've done, but I* *think it could be improved by adding more detail so the recommendations you suggest will result in action. Let me know if there's anything I can do to help you with that."*

How is this feedback constructive? It acknowledges your effort, identifies how the report can be improved without being accusatory, and shows support.

You: *"Thank you for pointing that out. I appreciate the chance to improve. I can see where adding more details would help make my report clearer and more actionable. I'd love to work on that and make sure my reports are exactly what you need."*

How is this response constructive? It shows openness, a willingness to learn, and appreciation for the constructive nature of the feedback. You've turned this feedback into an opportunity for growth.

Unfortunately, feedback isn't always delivered in a positive way. Sometimes it's delivered in an accusatory way, such as saying you're falling down on your job. Such feedback can make you feel defensive. How do you handle that feedback?

One option is to reframe it: "Thank you for sharing that; I always want to make sure my work supports the team effectively. Could you give me an example or point to specific areas where you'd like to see improvement? That way I can be sure to target those in my efforts going forward.

I'm happy to work on any adjustments to keep our high standards."

In this example, you've acknowledged the feedback, shown willingness to improve, and requested specific, actionable guidance. This helps steer the conversation toward solutions and demonstrates a positive attitude and a growth mindset.

You don't need to wait until someone gives you feedback. You can ask for it after making a presentation or completing a deliverable or some other work-related tasks. The more you ask for feedback and the more you're genuinely open to feedback in and out of the workplace, the more likely you'll receive it.

Feedback is just one aspect of communication. There are others that I'll briefly touch on since we communicate every day but there's always room for improvement, especially in the workplace.

Communication: Listening, Including Nonverbal Cues

Reading between the lines was the toughest part of my transition to the professional world. I didn't handle it well until a few years into my career. I learned the hard way.

—Pablo Lopez

What is Pablo referring to? I interpret his comment as the importance of listening for what is not being said.

When we listen, we do a few things. We remove distractions (like checking our cell phones), we show cues that we're listening (like nodding and leaning forward), we often paraphrase (such as restating or sharing a summary of what was said in your own words), and we ask open-ended questions (often beginning with what, why, or how, and not questions that result in a yes or no response). This is all about listening and listening actively to what was said.

Why is it also important to listen for what is not being said, not just what is said? People don't always communicate directly—they may be trying to be polite or avoiding an uncomfortable conversation. That's why reading between the lines is so important. For example, if I said "I'm feeling fine," but my tone is a painful whisper, you would question the honesty of my response. Certainly, listening for tone is one way of reading between the lines. Here are two other tips for reading between the lines.

1. **Notice body language.** Nonverbal cues such as crossed arms and avoiding direct eye contact reveal discomfort with a topic.

2. **Word choice.** Using words like "maybe" or "I guess" could mean avoiding commitment or signaling discomfort.

Developing the skill for understanding the potential layers underneath the spoken words is important. Asking clarifying questions or pointing out the discrepancy between the spoken word and tone (as in the example above) can uncover these additional layers. For example, you might indicate that you hear something is key for the other person but you want to understand more fully why it is key or what the history or context is.

However, it's also important not to over analyze. Some people do speak directly, and there isn't the need to read between the lines.

HR Pro Tip

Maximize the relationship you foster during and after work hours. This will come in handy, as people are often giving feedback about you in and outside of your presence.

Communication: Being Clear and Concise

Do you have a colleague or friend who speaks in para-graphs rather than in sentences? Do you have to listen very carefully to follow the point they are trying to make and not get lost in the details? Perhaps you do this your-self. I know I do at times. I try to edit the details of the story if I see my listener not paying attention. As with writing and speaking, especially in professional settings, you need to be clear and concise. Here are some tips to do this:

1. **Know your purpose.** Train yourself to know the main message you want to convey. Can you say or write it in one or two sentences?

2. **Use simple language.** Complicated words and long-winded expressions can lead to your target audience getting distracted.

3. **Shorten sentences.** Again, this helps the listener and reader follow along.

4. **Structure for clarity.** Is there a logic to your beginning, middle, and end? This helps the listener and reader follow along and anticipate what's to come. Maybe there are two or three key points you want to make. If so, begin by stating the number of points you'll be making; this will serve as the outline for your comments.

5. **Edit for clarity.** When writing, review what you've written and ask yourself if every word adds value. Is there redundancy? The redundancy question also applies to speaking.

Check out Chris Anderson's book on public speaking, which is listed in the Resources section.

Workplace Conduct

The way you address colleagues, communicate, and behave can open many doors as quickly as they can close them if you do not have proper etiquette.

—José Ricardo Ortiz

The quality of your work will greatly matter. So does how you conduct yourself, as José notes. In addition to the workplace culture and communication skills, knowing how to handle gossip and conflicts matters. This section focuses on conducting yourself and performing in a way that will advance your career.

Avoiding Gossip

Do not engage in workplace drama/gossip. Stay neutral.

—Kasia D.

You'll hear coworkers talking about others. A cardinal rule is avoiding gossip, as Kasia notes. What's a tactful way to do this? You can set boundaries by saying something like, "Let's get back to focusing on the task at hand." Another option is to counter whatever someone is negatively saying about a colleague with something positive. What if you're with a group of people and you can't steer the conversation away from the gossip? You can walk away and say something along the lines of "I've got to get back to my project." These approaches demonstrate to coworkers that you don't talk about people behind their backs. This can set a good example for others to do the same.

It's also important to avoid sharing personal information. If you're wondering if you can trust someone with your personal information or sensitive work information, it's a no. It's not worth the potential problems that can result.

You don't want to become the subject of gossip, and that's less likely to happen if you haven't given your coworkers something to gossip about.

The workplace is not like high school. You're not there to be popular; you're there to be a productive and collaborative colleague. Focus on the work at hand. This will help advance your career.

Handling Conflict

Disagreements will arise. Too often people feel trapped when there is a conflict—seeing the choices as all bad. It is a bad choice to ignore the conflict and hope it will go away. It is a bad choice to escalate the conflict in a contentious way. It is a bad choice to quit the job as a form of avoidance. So what do you do?

In some workplaces there is a culture of constructive engagement with conflict. For example, during a meeting people may invite constructive debate on an issue. They might say, "We should be hard on the issue, not each other." There may be an ombudsman office or human resources office where you can get coaching on how to handle conflict. There may be a grievance or complaint procedure where you can initiate a formal case with an investigation and a hearing. The same is true with legal avenues in cases of discrimination, harassment, and other rights that may have been violated. But most of the time, conflicts among coworkers or between workers and super-visors need to be resolved by those directly involved.

With coworker conflicts, an important tool in your tool kit is to discuss the process before you dive in on the issues. You might say, "We clearly disagree on this issue. Before going any further, let's make sure we understand what this is about for each of us. You go first—what are your con-cerns? I will try to summarize what I am hearing to make sure I'm hearing you correctly. If you could do the same for me, then we can explore options. Does that make sense?"

In many cases it's helpful to look beyond stated positions and surface underlying interests. A coworker might say to you, for example, "I haven't received your contributions to the report, which were due last week. As a result, we'll just have to go ahead without you." That is their position, but there are many possible underlying interests. It could be that your coworker is up against a deadline, your piece of the report is not that important, or they don't know what you're capable of doing. These are three very different rationales for the comment. Depending on the actual underlying interests, your response may be different. So what do you do? When confronted by a positional demand, ask questions: "I hear that you feel strongly—can you say more about what is at stake here? What might be some options so that I can help you be successful?" The goal is to convert a confrontation and conflict into a problem-solv-ing conversation.

The bottom line is that conflict is inevitable in a workplace where people are interdependent and have a complex mix of goals and circumstances. Conflict will happen—the question is what you will do with it. Your mission should be to engage in a constructive conversation rather than being conflict avoidant or escalating the issue. Often, once you and others fully understand the issues and the underlying interests, solutions can be found that will address the challenges in a way that is acceptable to everyone.

Conflicts between you and your supervisor are different than conflicts between you and coworkers. In some cases, the responsibility lies with the supervisor who lacks the needed skills. In those cases, one option is to manage up, which means helping the supervisor to be more constructive. For example, don't go toe-to-toe but listen and restate what you hear your supervisor saying and also offer another option. In other cases, you may want to seek advice from a mentor familiar with the situation. Ultimately, the situation is complicated by the power difference in terms of formal authority.

A good question to ask yourself when there are power differences is, "What other sources of power do I have?" For example, there is power that comes from creative solutions; there is power that comes from coworkers; there is power that comes from constructive

> **HR Pro Tip**
>
> *There are many company resources that can assist with conflict management. Contacting your EAP and/or HR can help.*

influence through other channels; and there is power that comes with access to useful information.

There is also conflict that can arise with race, class, and gender dimensions.

> *I realized that students coming out of college will make mistakes, so they need good mentors to help them grow professionally. In my experience, people of color don't always get a lot of chances to make mistakes. You are sometimes expected to get things right the first time or you're expected to fail. I wasn't always given grace or room for growth like my White colleagues who also made rookie mistakes. I also was not matched with the right mentors in my corporate jobs. I needed a mentor who would affirm me and give me professional advice to help me navigate my challenges.*
>
> —Chelsa Moore

It's very possible that there are issues of race, gender, or class going on. It's also possible that it's just a substantive issue that happens to involve people of different races, genders, or classes. One of the hardest things to do is to figure out which of these scenarios is occurring. Essentially, you're in a position of formulating a hypothesis and testing it. For example, if you think you're being treated unfairly, like Chelsa, you can test that hypothesis. Does the manager's behavior happen consistently with you and others like you? If so, do gentle nudges help shift the behavior? Ask questions such as "Does this apply in all cases?" If there is a discriminatory pattern, then formal channels discussed above may be needed. These can include discussing your experience with an ombudsman, the HR department, a mentor, or others.

Often, you won't encounter direct discrimination but what people call microaggressions. For example, two people may make similar comments, and one is recognized and the other is ignored. One way of countering microaggressions is to reflect back on what people are saying or doing in a non-blaming way. Just putting a spotlight on the statement or behavior ("I hear you saying . . .") can often lead to a reduction in the problematic comments or behaviors. Of course, you can directly counter the statement with evidence if you are comfortable doing so (even given power or status differences). A deeper strategy to counter microaggressions is through what a leading ombudsman, Mary Rowe, calls microaffirmations. That is, reinforcing positive behaviors when they happen, which slowly helps change the culture. More about recognizing and handling microaggressions can be found in the Resources section.

Stay versus Go

As already illustrated in this chapter, I have too often seen former students entering the workforce and feeling there is no alternative to solving a conflict or serious misstep other than leaving. This often happens within the first year, when learning about the culture, the job, coworkers, and themselves are intertwined. Leaving a position is a big deal. At the minimum, think about the time and energy involved in searching for, securing, and proving yourself in a new position.

As author Tessa White writes, "When it comes to deciding to stay or go, speed is the enemy."

Before you make a deliberate, nonemotional decision to leave your job, take the time to consider the pros and cons of your choices (not just stay versus go, but perhaps another choice is stay and pivot). Also, honestly understand *why* your current position isn't working for you and what you need in your next role. You don't want to repeat the pattern in future roles. Dig deeper than using a catchall phrase like "It was a toxic environment." In her book *The Unspoken Truths for Career Success*, White recommends a value analysis, comparing your values to your organization's values on these dimensions: growth/learning, flexibility, risk, autonomy, and connection. There could be other values for comparing, too. In doing this values analysis, it should give you deeper personal insight. In the end, after thoughtful consideration, only you can determine if you need to exit your role.

Resiliency

When I got accepted to Illinois, the dean of my entire high school told me that the only reason I got accepted was because I was Brown. Hearing those words from him hurt quite a bit. I took a step back, and I said, "Well, sir, I'd like to think it was my strong GPA and who I am as a person, the stature I have in my family, and you know all that good stuff and the fact that I've been able to succeed given a lot of the different things I'm dealing with." At that point I had four siblings I was taking care of when my parents worked. I had almost a 4.0 out of a 4.5 GPA, played football all four years, ran track two years; I was on student council all four years and involved with the Spanish club. That shows you my level of leadership and involvement. That comment from the dean was the backbone when my motivation began . . . being told you're not good enough. And the only reason you are good enough is because of the color of your skin.

—Tony V.

The dean's misguided comment could have resulted in Tony seriously questioning his abilities despite his strong academic and extracurricular performance while in high school. Instead it did the opposite. It fueled Tony's motivation. His resilience then and at other times in his career, like when he later lost his position and had to temporarily move back to his mother's home, made him even more motivated to succeed.

You might know people like Tony who maintain a positive outlook despite the stress and setbacks in life. If you're like them, it's a gift. Perhaps it comes naturally. If not, here are some tips that may help you learn to become more resilient when you're faced with work (and life) challenges.

1. **Name your emotions.** When you experience a setback, what emotion or set of emotions do you feel? Are you angry, embarrassed, ashamed, or feeling something else? Identify the feelings and see if you can let them go. Understanding what you're feeling can help you manage your emotions. There's a link to an exercise video in the Resources section that can help you do this.

2. **Break down problems.** A setback like not securing a major account can feel like a big problem. Instead of ruminating about it over and over again, try breaking down the plausible reasons why you didn't land the account and develop an action plan for moving forward. This can help you feel more in control of the situation.

3. **Learn from setbacks.** Think about an important lesson you learned. Did the lesson emerge from making a mistake or experiencing something unfortunate outside of your control? Train yourself to consistently reframe mistakes, roadblocks, and disappointments as a chance to grow and improve. As Nelson Mandela said, "I never lose. I either win or learn."

4. **Practice positivity.** Embodying an attitude of gratitude is one way to practice positivity. Another

is visualizing success, even small successes like leaving a good impression on your new supervisor. You'll like yourself better and others will, too.

5. **Take care of yourself.** What makes a child happy? As adults we're not that much different from children. Make sure you regularly get a good night's sleep, feed your body with the nutrition it needs, prioritize exercise, and also be nourished through close friendships. Taking care of yourself will make you feel more stable when faced with life's inevitable challenges.

6. **Know your purpose.** Why do you do what you do? Is it out of loyalty, keeping your word, wanting to make a difference in the world, or something else? Knowing and reminding yourself of your values can serve as a source of motivation for why you're persevering when encountering setbacks.

Building resiliency is possible, but give yourself grace. It takes time and consistent effort. Start small and gradually incorporate these practices into your life to see long-term benefits.

Adaptability and Growth Mindset

Be open to pivoting and open to all possibilities. You never know what doors can and will open for you.

—Kevin Collins

Your career isn't a straight line and shouldn't be. Anticipate change as that is how you will grow. Take opportunities that may scare you or make you uncomfortable.

—Magdala Boyer

The Greek philosopher Heraclitus is quoted as saying, "Change is the only constant in life." In the workplace, this rings especially true—your office mate, your boss, your clients, and your assignments are all likely to change over time. That's why adaptability isn't just helpful; it's essential. Kevin and Magdala embrace it. Do you?

Assess how adaptable you are by answering these questions:

1. How do I respond to sudden changes?

2. Am I comfortable with ambiguity?

3. How willing am I to learn new skills or take on tasks outside my comfort zone?

4. Am I open to new ideas, even if they challenge my current ways of thinking or working?

What did you learn about yourself by reflecting on your answers to these questions? Are you more rigid or are you strong enough to bend?

Being adaptable is part of a growth mindset. That is, you believe you can expand what you know and what you can do. This type of mindset leads to overall achievement. Companies count on their employees to adapt to changing environments in order to remain competitive. You don't escape this requirement in the nonprofit sector.

The opposite of a growth mindset is a rigid or fixed mindset. This is when you believe your natural talents can't be improved, that you can't change—*this is just who I am.* This mindset often leads to avoiding challenges for fear of failure and viewing constructive criticism as a personal attack rather than as an opportunity to learn and grow. You can imagine how having a fixed mindset leads to all kinds of personal and professional challenges.

A few things already mentioned in chapter 6 (continuous learning) and in this chapter (seeking feedback and building resiliency) help you become more adaptable and are illustrative of having a growth mindset. Here are a few more tips:

1. **Practice flexibility in problem-solving.** There's typically more than one way to solve a problem. Developing alternative approaches can increase your cognitive flexibility. This helps you move away from rigid, single-solution thinking and encourages you to innovate and adapt when necessary.

2. **Build collaborative skills.** Your willingness to share responsibilities fosters teamwork. This may also involve adjusting or adapting your

approach to meet the strengths and weaknesses of your colleagues.

3. **Know your blind spots.** What do others see that you don't? Every strength has a corresponding limitation—knowing what you are not good at helps make you more open to input from others.

Work Quality

Worth comes from the quality of work. As long as you produce, that is what my firm cares about. I really don't think being non-White played a role or impacted me negatively in any way. I live my life being respectful. That is my mindset and fortunately it has worked out.

—Brian F.

Do you know what's expected of you at work? Your job description should be a guide, but it probably doesn't include the key performance indicators (KPIs) on which you are being evaluated. Brian, a lawyer, produces billable hours from clients. In order to have billable hours, he needs to meet client needs, whatever they might be. There's no doubt that he aims to meet or exceed the expected number of billable hours each month. That's a clear performance metric.

In meeting or exceeding expectations at work, it's important to know the KPIs on which you're being evaluated. One general way to gather this information, such as during an interview, is to ask, "If I'm fantastically successful, what will that look like at the end of my first year?" In the response, you'll hear what really matters in your role and what you need to make sure you focus on. A specific way of asking this question once you're in your job is, "what are the key performance indicators (KPIs) on which I'll be evaluated?" Perhaps this will be an indicator that's clearly measurable, such as billable hours. But perhaps it's more interpretive, such as "submitting quality work." If the latter is the case, spend a bit of mental energy to gain clarity on what *quality* is within your work context. For example, is submitting quality work a report that requires no edits? Is it a report that is delivered on time and within budget?

Another suggestion is to ask if your organization has a standard form that is used to complete employee evaluations. If so, review it with your supervisor and ask if there are examples of behaviors that would be coded as exemplary versus adequate in each category or performance indicator that you'll be evaluated on.

In addition to the KPIs, it's also constructive to think about the process for doing your work. Here are two examples:

I'm coming to work, and I'm almost on time every day, like I'm getting there right on the clock. But I'm rushing. Nobody's saying anything to me. Then I thought, Why do you need someone to say anything to you for you to get to work and to have enough time to settle into your role?

Just because someone isn't saying anything doesn't mean it's not noticed. It's learning to take accountability and responsibility for yourself.

—J. M.

Be a team player. Helping others and showing your coworkers how supportive you are is really beneficial in advancing your career.

—Ashton Keola

J. M. learned that being ready to work, and not just arriving on time, was an unstated expectation. For Ashton, it wasn't just being collaborative with coworkers on completing assignments but also supporting them in their roles that was noticed by others, which led to more opportunities. These examples of being ready to work and not just arriving to work on time and being a team player wouldn't be listed as KPIs, but they are noticeable and do matter for navigating and advancing your career.

Delivering quality work is never a one-time thing. It is a continuous process. Perhaps your workplace has a quality or continuous improvement program. These are formal processes through which all workers are encouraged to make and help implement improvement suggestions. If there is such a program, it is good to know at the outset. If there isn't, you may find that there is interest in starting one!

Self-Advocacy

Sometimes you can excel in the process of completing your work as well as meeting or exceeding the KPIs, but it doesn't lead to promotions. This happened to Manuel.

> *Hard work alone won't speak for itself. You must advocate for yourself and own your success. Don't expect promotions and pay raises to come to you without any effort.*

> —Manuel Gomez

Manuel, as well as other first-gen alums, spoke about working hard and producing quality of work but not having a supervisor recommend them for a promotion. They eventually learned to advocate for themselves. Some first-gens, especially women, may have been told in the past to not stand out and to not toot your own horn. In the world of work, not advocating for yourself is counterproductive. Here are a few tips on how to prepare to advocate for yourself:

1. **Document achievements.** Quantify your achievements to the greatest extent possible. For example, "I brought in three more clients beyond my KPI each month for the past year, which resulted in annual revenue growth of $500,000." State how this aligns with the company's goals.

2. **Track praise.** Collect notes of appreciation or praise from customers, colleagues, or partners within your

industry. Keep them in a file that you can share with your supervisor as further documentation of your performance.

3. **Take initiative.** Volunteer for projects that help you grow as a professional. This demonstrates leadership potential and should align with your vision for your career goals. In addition, choose projects that will allow you to come into direct contact with people at the top of your organization. Let them come to know (and literally see) who you are!

4. **Know what you want.** Are you looking to increase your salary based on your current role and responsibilities? Or do you want a salary increase with a new job title and expanded responsibilities? Either way, do your research and know your value. Research what employees in these roles get paid when working for a competitor. Glassdoor and Indeed are two online resources that offer compensation calculators, and you may also filter beyond title and city to include such factors as education and years of experience. Talking with peers in similar roles is also a resource for understanding salary parameters.

Ask to schedule a meeting with your supervisor once you're prepared. Let your supervisor know in advance what the meeting is about. For example, you could say, "I'd like to talk with you about my past performance and opportunities to continue contributing to the company."

As the meeting begins, express gratitude for the opportunities you've experienced to date and state that you'd like to discuss being promoted. This is where you can bring in your prepared work. You could say, for example, "I've thoroughly

HR Pro Tip

No matter how the conversation goes, always mention growth opportunities as an area of focus on your annual performance review.

enjoyed working for you at [Company] for the past year. During this time, I've [state achievements]. I have a file of the appreciation notes I've received from colleagues and partners based on these achievements if you'd like to see it. (Have this file with you.) You know I've also shown initiative by [state examples] and [benefits realized]. Going forward, I'd like to take on more responsibility by [explicitly state projects] and receive fair compensation for these efforts." Pause and let your supervisor respond to you. If the reaction is positive, then transition the conversation by stating your preferred position title, additional responsibilities, and salary expectations.

Always have your best alternative to a negotiated agreement (BATNA) in mind. For example, you'd like a management position and learned a fair compensation is [$XX]. At the same time, you might have a mental note to yourself that you'd settle for an associate management position for [$XX] with an opportunity to reopen the conversation in six months. This fallback option would be your BATNA.

Salary increases matter. Small increases in pay add up to sizable differences in lifetime earnings. For example, if two people started off making the same amount of money but their annual increases over thirty-five years were 2 percent vs 5 percent lifetime earnings would be close to double below.

Example Tim v Tina	Timid Tim	Trekking Tina
Starting salary	$50,000	$50,000
Years worked	40	40
Average raise %	2%	5%
Total in lifetime earnings	$3,020,099	$6,039,989

And finally, when advocating for yourself, keep in mind this advice from Manuel:

Whenever you are promised something or given a commitment, especially when related to career growth opportunities, pay, work conditions, etcetera, it always need to be formally documented. At the very least it should be sent via email so it can be referenced with a time stamp. I've seen at least one coworker not get a promotion they were promised because their supervisor had left the organization and the commitment to the promotion was not documented anywhere.

—Manuel Gomez

Goal Setting

Be proactive in seeking growth opportunities, acquiring new skills, and aligning your career path with your aspirations over time. Remember, career advancement is often a gradual process of continuous improvement and adaptation.

—Keshav Regmi

Having goals gives direction, motivation, and a clear sense of purpose, allowing you to steer your career intentionally. This is what Keshav does and it's his advice to other first-gen alums like him.

One effective framework for goal setting is creating SMART goals. The acronym stands for **s**pecific, **m**easurable, **a**chievable, **r**elevant, and **t**ime-bound. A SMART goal is illustrated below through an example that might be relevant to you as you graduate and begin your career.

Goal: Develop a professional network within my industry to identify potential mentors and learning opportunities over the next six months.

Specific: Begin building a professional network in my industry by connecting with professionals through my university's alumni network and on LinkedIn, having at least one informational interview per week (video or in person), attending at least one industry event each month, and identifying at least two potential mentors by the end of six months.

Notice this is a well-defined goal that answers the who, what, when, and where.

Measurable: Create an Excel spreadsheet to track the number of new connections made (and through what source), how many one-on-one informational meetings took place, and the number of times you reached out to potential mentors, and if the outreach was successful.

Notice metrics are identified to track goal progress.

Achievable: Dedicate one to two hours per week to networking activities noted above.

Notice the goal is challenging but feasible.

Relevant: Building a network is crucial for my career growth as a first-gen graduate. It will help me learn from experienced professionals, gain industry insights, and access potential new opportunities.

Notice the goal is integral to a larger plan and answers the why question.

Time-bound: Complete the goal within six months, with a check-in every month to assess progress and adjust my approach as necessary.

Notice the goal has a deadline and room for midcourse corrections if needed.

You could leave it as an overarching goal (stated initially) without going through the SMART steps, but do you think you would be as focused, accountable, and achieve the goal? Doubtful, right?

Goal setting is a mindset, not just a task. It involves aspiring to accomplish something, knowing where you are now, and charting a path to get from here to there. Goals will change based on having been accomplished or needing adjustment due to new information or new circumstances. Still, at any point in time, you should have key goals top of mind. These can be periodically reviewed with your mentor or supervisor.

Navigating a Bad Fit

A mentor told me that I should ideally be earning and learning at a job. It's okay if you are only earning or learning but if you don't have either it's time to move on. I was very disheartened that my first job was neither. I didn't feel like people cared what I did and didn't feel my work was important. This was really hard on me after spending all of college worrying and working hard to get a good job after school. If you can avoid it, move on from a company before you don't like working at the company anymore. If you don't like your work, the job will drain all your energy. You won't have the energy to apply to other roles after work.

—Grace B.

Having goals will help give you career direction but what if you're like Grace, where you accept a position and soon learn it wasn't what you thought it would be? The position is simply not a fit. It's probably going to be a short-lived position, but that's okay. You'll have learned from the experience what you don't like, which sometimes is just as important as realizing what you do like.

The risk of accepting any position, rather than waiting for a position that's a good fit, is greater for first-gen alums. This is because we typically don't have a strong safety net.

As it's a safe assumption that you need a position to pay bills and not just for personal fulfillment, do everything possible to secure a new position while you're still working. Why is this the case? First, you have bills to pay and probably haven't yet saved for your emergency fund. Second, you are more likely to be hired for a position while still employed. This is because being employed signals to hiring managers that you're a valuable candidate. They are likely to assume you have up-to-date skills and are in good standing with your current role. Third, as an employed candidate, you'll tend to negotiate with more leverage and confidence since you're not under pressure to take any job.

This is the best advice. However, I've known former students who are in such unbearable situations that they quit before securing another position. They don't have much of a safety net and it's tough. They might soon be underemployed, which means accepting a position that doesn't require a college degree, until they find a position that is more suitable to them. During a robust economy, this approach carries risk but the risk is much greater during recessionary times.

One additional fact worth repeating is research shows that if college graduates are initially underemployed, they are significantly more likely to be underemployed ten years after college. This is especially the case for women and people who don't work in the technology sector.

So what does this all mean?

Navigating a career always takes place on two levels— the practical level and the as-pirational level. If you're making career decisions for prac-tical reasons (paying the bills, being limited by geography, etc.), acknowledge that. Have a parallel plan to generate aspirational options. That can include carving out time for informational interviews with people in aspirational roles, learning more about aspirational employers, and building skills that will be valued in the aspirational work.

> **HR Pro Tip**
>
> *It is okay to have a gap in your employment; just be prepared to provide a sound rationale for the gap in a cover letter and/ or during an interview process.*

At the same time, don't drop the ball on the practical work— sometimes what you thought as a more limited practical job can evolve in unexpected ways. Even if it doesn't, rec-ommendations by former managers matter. So do a great job of being where you are, while also positioning yourself for where you want to go.

What if you view each challenge as an opportunity to advance your career? Why not keep striving for what's next?

CHAPTER 8

WORK-LIFE BALANCE

Work-life balance helps me perform better on the job. There are breaks in college, it's a marathon at work.

—Manuel Gomez

Work-life balance, meaning finding ways to manage the demands of your work with the things that are important to you in your personal life, hasn't always been a thing. The roots of the idea began with the Labor Movement at the turn of the early twentieth century when unions pushed for the eight-hour workday, an end to child labor, and workplace safety. The underlying concepts gained momentum during the feminist movement over fifty years ago with increasing numbers of women entering the workforce and having to juggle home and family responsibilities. Work-life balance became a term in the 1980s as companies began experimenting with flexible work arrangements and later with the government's passage of the Family Medical Leave Act (FLMA). Subsequently, following the rise of technology and the internet, work-life boundaries became increasingly blurred. The ideal of balance became harder to achieve for many. More recently, with COVID-19, these boundaries became even more challenging as the home also became the workplace.

Work-life balance involves more than just caring for aging parents and young children—though these are critical life cycle realities. Stress and mental health are gaining added importance as factors in discussing work-life balance.

In our survey, 37 percent of men and 22 percent of women gave work-life balance advice. Remember, these are first-gen alums who are about ten years out since graduating.

One thing I would have done differently is just gone home. I work in tech. I'm not a heart surgeon or brain surgeon. Right? I'm not saving lives. I'm building or supporting, servicing a software. At the end of the day, just go home and be home, be present. That's still something I struggle with, because now I work from home. My home is my work. Where is the line? When do I take off the advertising operations hat and become Tony the husband, the dog dad, and the homeowner? I should have built that rigor early on.

—Tony V.

I began working with a celebrity and his family as a nanny/tutor. The role quickly turned into a multi-faceted role where I also took on the responsibilities as an executive assistant/ coordinator. The physical, emotional, and mental demands of the job became all-encompassing, and it was very difficult to draw the line and balance a personal and work life.

—Tiffany Remington

It probably isn't uncommon for first-generation college grads entering the workforce, like Tony and Tiffany, to prove themselves by working long hours, skipping meals, and having little to no personal time. If you're like Tony and Tiffany, you're excited to start your position, you want to do an outstanding job, and then after a period of time, you start to feel burned out. Perhaps you're feeling tired and anxious, and not motivated or focused. These feelings and symptoms aren't due to a bad week; the feelings are persistent and longer lasting. (See chapter 3 for more information about burnout.)

This doesn't happen to every person working long and demanding hours. Some people live to work and enjoy every minute of it. You might know someone in their seventies still working as if they were in their fifties. Work gives them life; it fulfills them. However, research suggests we get less productive and creative when we work long hours[vi].

Perhaps you love your work but also love your dog or drawing or playing on the local baseball team. If you envision or crave work-life balance, here's some advice from first-gen alums.

Setting Boundaries

A business partner in his 70s said to me, "Have you thought when enough is enough? You need to make sure you have a good work-life balance. One day you're going to have kids who will need you." I really appreciate that he took the time to just remind me that I don't have to work all the time, because it's easy to hit the ground running and just keep going.

—Brian F.

Brian had permission from someone in authority who recognized his hard work. This certainly makes it easier to periodically cut back on the workload when needed to balance out other important personal responsibilities and aspects of your life.

But what if you're the only one who seems to be feeling out of balance? Everyone else is arriving early, working through lunch, staying late, answering emails on weekends. How do you set boundaries when you are feeling the strain and don't have internal role models and certainly not permission from someone in authority?

Learn the power of no.

—Shanicka S. Burdine

If you don't have primary caregiving responsibilities, it might feel hard to say no. What's your excuse if everyone else is plugging along and saying yes? Shanicka fits this category yet recommends learning the power of no. A key way to do this is by clarifying your role, responsibilities, and related expectations with your manager. How does this help? It can prevent you from taking on tasks beyond what is expected. It helps you to say no, as Shanicka advises.

If saying no feels too definitive for you, perhaps "not now" is a better approach for the time being. This illustrates that your platter is now full but you'd still like to be able to contribute when you have capacity to do so. If you use "not now" to set a boundary, make sure you do come back when you have the capacity or when the issues match your role. The rule of thumb is to prioritize tasks that are aligned with your job responsibilities and your professional goals, all while staying within limits that keep you from burning out.

Here are some other ways to set boundaries:

1. **Stick to your defined work hours.** Communicate with others who you work with so they know when you are and are not available. Treat exceptions as exceptions—you can stretch hours in a crisis situation but not every day.

2. **Take regular breaks.** Use your lunch period; don't work at your desk during lunch. How about walking and eating lunch or meeting with a colleague or friend to enjoy a nonwork-related conversation? And vacation days are there for a reason. Use them—you certainly don't want to lose them.

3. **Prioritize tasks and be realistic.** What's urgent? What can wait? Are you taking on tasks that are unrelated to your goals? You should be able to tell. Are the tasks all within your control so you have a clear sense of what's involved and the realistic timeline to completion? Or is there the potential for bottlenecks, where you need to rely on others for input or approval before the task is fully completed? If there's the potential for bottle-necks, build this into your work plan and timeline, as it will impact your workflow. Sometimes it's about not working harder but working smarter.

4. **Learn to delegate.** If you're working in a team, play to the strengths of other team members to even out the workload. Consider using an Eisenhower Matrix (see chapter 3). No one team member should feel overwhelmed.

5. **Ask for assistance.** If you're not working in a team or have authority to delegate, ask your boss for temporary help to meet deadlines and share in the work responsibilities.

6. **If working remotely, define your workspace.** If you don't have a dedicated office in your home for work, most likely you'll be working at a table where you also eat or at a chair where you also watch TV or read a book. If this is your reality, your defined workspace is where your laptop lands. Consider a true boundary to your workday

by logging out of your computer, changing into some after-work clothes, and taking a quick walk outside before "coming home from work." Do your best not to read your work emails or text messages after you put your laptop away. If you feel compelled to look at them, only respond to those that are true emergencies.

Your workplace culture, based on the company's policies, should influence if you experience a work-life balance. If work-life balance is important to you, here are some questions to ask during the interview process (if the answers aren't provided in the job posting):

1. Are there flexible working hours?

2. Are there remote work options?

3. Are there paid time off policies and, if so, are they mandatory?

4. Are there on-site wellness programs, employee assistance programs, and caregiver support programs?

5. Is there a policy that limits when meetings, texting, or Slacking begin and end during the workday?

If the answer is yes to any of these questions, policies are in place that aim for work-life balance. However, just keep in mind that despite the policies, actual workplace practices might differ. For example, there might be paid time off, but coworkers rarely take it. Or meetings aren't supposed to be scheduled before 8:00 a.m., but you've been invited to several that begin at 7:30 a.m. As noted above, it will be your responsibility to create boundaries for your own well-being if the work culture doesn't.

Self-Care and Self-Reflection

Continue to make time for and check in with yourself outside of work to make sure you're taking care of yourself in a holistic way.

—Victoria L.

How might you check in with yourself, as Victoria recommends? One way is by paying attention to your body. Is your breathing erratic or measured? Do you feel tension? Are you feeling low energy? Are you in control of the tone in which you're speaking? Another way is by honestly asking yourself questions. Do you ever ask yourself what's going on right now in your head? Do you question what's causing you stress or joy?

Self-reflection and self-care are closely linked. The more you recognize your emotions, patterns, and needs, the more effective you can be in caring for yourself.

It might be helpful to share my own work-life balance story, even though I'm of an older generation. Up until the time I had my first child, my work was my primary identity. I loved what I did and the impact I was making. I was promoted to direct research and planning for a cabinet-level state agency when I was twenty-six years old. It never felt like I was close to being burned out. However, when I became pregnant, I worried that my work would be all-consuming and I wouldn't get to know my child. It wasn't that my work-place was putting demands on me—it was me putting demands on myself. To protect myself from this, I requested to work part-time. While part-time work was never really part-time (again, because of me and how I work), it gave me the flexibility for professional engagement while raising my two sons and being fully present in their lives.

Here's another example. One of my first-gen colleagues loved her work as a university professor. After getting promoted and tenured (which is lifetime employment unless something egregious happens), she learned that she would have significant additional work responsibilities without additional administrative support to help her with this. Worried that she would eventually burn out, she decided to change jobs and began working at a nonprofit organization where she envisioned greater work-life balance. Guess what? It didn't happen! Once again she was faced with increasing work responsibilities coupled with long work hours at an organization she loved. This repeating pattern helped her recognize that everywhere she went, there she was. She realized that it was truly her responsibility to set work limits despite the fact that many of her colleagues were working as many, if not more, hours.

Why do I tell these stories? Because it involves knowing yourself. Not all work-life balance woes can be blamed on the workplace.

I find it interesting that mental health is now integral to work-life balance considerations. Are technology, the internet, and workplace arrangements post-COVID the main reasons for this? Is it that mental health challenges are less taboo or is there an increase in mental illness? Is it that there are generational differences? Is it that employers and employees are less loyal to each other? Is it that companies focus less on how jobs are designed, leading to work overload? Whatever the reasons, work-life balance, including mental health, is real. Self-care and self-reflection are advised.

In chapter 7, I wrote that as adults we have similar needs that we had as children (proper nutrition, a good night's sleep, exercise, time to socialize). These are baseline life tasks for self-care and are expanded on a bit more below.

1. **Nutrition**—How do you feel when you eat properly? Do you have more energy? Do you think clearer? It should be no surprise that there is a link between nutrition and well-being. The healthy food we eat provides the nutrients our body needs for growth and repair. We've been taught about the importance of fruits, vegetables, healthy fats, lean protein, dairy, and whole grains in our diets for years. More recently, we've been reminded to hydrate. And we need to think

about how we eat. Are we being mindful or are we rushing? How would you rate your nutritional habits? In what ways might there be room for improvement?

2. **Sleep**—Similar to work-life balance, sleep is important. There's technology to track our sleeping patterns, and there's a link between sleep and so many aspects of our awake life, such as our moods, our cognitive health, and our physical health. When we sleep, it's a restorative process that enables our bodies and minds to perform at their best. The amount of recommended sleep we need varies by age, but between the ages of eighteen and sixty-four, anywhere from seven to nine hours of sleep is recommended each night. How are you faring on the sleep front? Is this something you prioritize and achieve? (See Resources section for an additional reading on the topic.)

3. **Exercise**—Did you know the minimum amount of moderate exercise recommended by the US Department of Health and Human Services is 150 minutes per week plus two muscle strengthening workouts? Moderate exercise includes things such as playing doubles tennis, walking, or even doing household chores. How are you getting in your minimum 150 minutes of exercise? Is your preference to get into a daily routine or to do longer workouts a few times a week? Whatever

works for you, the point is to make exercise an integral part of your lifestyle.

4. **Socialization**—Socialization is a fundamental human need that supports nearly every aspect of our lives. The degree of socialization varies based on each of our needs. Meaningful social connections create a sense of belonging and are essential for our overall well-being and longevity. Think about how often you reach out to talk with a friend when you have a concern to discuss, an accomplishment to share, or just to lend a listening ear and bring with you a caring heart. We need our friends. How do you build socialization into your life and maintain meaningful social connections?

> **HR Pro Tip**
>
> *Check your company benefits! Many medical plans offer discounts on gym memberships and wellness incentives.*

What additional self-care options might you need? Determining this requires you to reflect on your emotional patterns and what has worked to meet your needs in the past.

Here are a few more relevant and noteworthy quotes from first-gen alums.

Remember that your job is only one aspect of who you are.

—Chaz S.

I wish I took my work less seriously. I don't mean that I wish I worked less. I mean that I wish I didn't anchor my worth based on the results of my output. I thought my achievements, accolades, and LinkedIn profile defined who I was. I worked hard but at the cost of cynicism and burnout. I'm learning now how to give my best for the sake of doing "good work" rather than for self-validation.

—Yohan Ko

Both Chaz and Yohan are saying the same thing but in different ways. Their advice is to remember you're a whole person and the other nonwork parts of you are valuable, too. And Jarron's point below has validity, especially when you start feeling out-of-balance.

Treat yourself to recall that you've done a good job. You are a success. You've come from challenging places to be where you are at. That's not arrogant, that's not cocky; it's okay to say I did a good job or I did something valuable even if no one else notices or sees it; treat yourself and be appreciative of the work that you bring.

—Jarron F.

What if you prioritized your well-being as much as your work? Why not create a balance that lets you thrive in both?

CONCLUDING THOUGHTS ON FIRST-GEN IDENTITY

Did you move into your dorm by yourself while your roommate had the help of her mom? Perhaps you stayed on campus during breaks while others vacationed. Maybe a study abroad trip introduced you to classmates who casually compared their parents' high-powered jobs while you grew up with your grandmother.

Being a first-generation college graduate often, though not always, means coming from a low-income background. College may have been the first time you noticed financial disparities between yourself and your peers. These class differences don't vanish after graduation—they continue into the workplace (even if you are the highest earner in your family) and beyond.

Here are five different scenarios I or other first-gen college grads encountered after graduating from college. Approaches for handling these types of scenarios follow.

Scenario 1A: I completed my undergraduate degree at a regional college in four years while working almost full-time throughout those four years. I immediately started graduate school at a different state school with a grant that covered all my educational costs. It was in graduate school that I met my future husband. Upon graduation, we married and then relocated to Cambridge, Massachusetts, where my husband began graduate studies. I was casually asked by a new acquaintance from an Ivy League doctoral program where I went to college. After I told her, she replied that I would never find work in Boston coming from Midwest regional schools. Note: She never learned I was offered two fantastic positions within two weeks and within one year, at the age of twenty-six, was promoted to direct research and planning for a cabinet-level state agency.

> **My reaction at the time:** Shock. Did I just hear what I thought she said? I said nothing but thought, *Well, she doesn't know me!* Her words stayed with me because I had been proud of being the first in my family to graduate, and it never occurred to me that my degrees would be perceived as less valuable than others simply because of where I earned them.

Scenario 1B: While Scenario 1A was decades ago, 1B occurred recently. It was at a dinner party. Everyone attending was in their 60s. The conversations were wide reaching and everyone was engaging. At one point, the conversation turned not only to where we went to college but where our parents and grandparents went to college. For everyone else at the table, it was at some of the country's most recognizable schools—Brown, Cornell,

Harvard, Princeton, MIT, and University of Pennsylvania. When it was my turn to share, I sensed judgment from a person sitting near me. This was despite just talking about supporting former college students to finish their degrees.

My reaction at the time: In addition to sensing judgment versus curiosity or inspiration, it reinforced how important for some people their alma mater is to their identity—even decades after graduating.

Scenario 2: After my friend John graduated from college, he secured a position in a city where he initially knew no one except the person who hired him. Through someone in his apartment building who was launching a new restaurant, he met a small group of friends who had more financial resources than he had. These friends could afford dinners out and expensive weekend trips. Rather than saying he didn't have the money to join in on the various social activities, John charged these expenses to his high interest credit card. He could barely pay the minimum credit card balance each month. This spending beyond his means negatively impacted his credit score.

What happened to John: Though uncomfortable, he started declining invites from his moneyed friends, saying he couldn't afford to participate. This didn't mean his friendship with them ended—it just meant he couldn't join them for everything they invited him to do. Also, he got involved with causes that were important to him that didn't require spending money, which allowed him to make an additional circle of friends.

Scenario 3: Another first-gen friend, Mary, was in her fifth year as an assistant professor. Her teaching evaluations were solid, she was awarded research grants, she published her research in scholarly journals, and she participated in service work for her university—all activities that mattered for getting promoted. Despite these successes, she questioned whether or not she fit in as an academic. She felt judged by her peers because of her working class background. At one point, her program came under fire and she faced a choice: Does she lean in to the battle over saving the program (and thus her position) or take a more secure position in a different sector? She chose the security of working in an organization where her working-class background was an asset.

> **What happened to Mary:** While Mary opted out of academia and began working in an environment that was a better match for her sense of self and values, most positions are not stable. There are no guarantees. She has had to relocate a couple of times over the past fifteen years because of job losses and opportunities.

Scenario 4: While attending a conference for a nonprofit association, I was invited to dinner with a group of about fifteen other attendees. Since the association didn't cover meal expenses, I knew I'd be paying out of pocket, so I kept it simple—just soup and water. The rest of the group ordered wine, appetizers, entrées, and dessert. When the bill arrived, the person who invited me suggested splitting it evenly to make it easier for the server. My fifteen-dollar soup suddenly cost me $125.

My reaction at the time: I felt uncomfortable asking for my bill to be separate considering the peer pressure to split the one bill. My takeaway lesson was to be cautious about joining large groups of people for dinner or to ask the server up front for a separate bill.

Scenario 5: Despite having a college degree, Leo's mom, Lenore, lacked the flexibility in her job that many other parents enjoyed. She couldn't take time off for school events, volunteer opportunities, or committee meetings; she could only afford to step away from work for essential parent-teacher conferences. In contrast, other parents, though also working, held jobs with more flexibility, allowing them to be visibly engaged in school activities and easily connect with one another. This difference in work flexibility left Lenore and Leo on the margins of the school community, missing out on valuable social connections and support.

What happened to Lenore and Leo: Things didn't change for Lenore. She still doesn't have a position that allows for flexibility, but she has a roof over her head and is able to provide for her son. She finds meaning in her relationship with her church and her son. Leo was able to graduate from college on an athletic scholarship and is beginning his career based on his own talent and resources, not intergenerational wealth and family connections that have been afforded to other friends he met along the way.

Here are three approaches to consider when issues of class arise in the workplace or in life:

1. **Reflect and name the feeling you're experiencing.** Are you feeling surprised (like me in the conversations with the new acquaintances), embarrassed (like John with an inability to say no to expensive invites), inferior (like Mary in her academic job), resentment (like me at the restaurant), or disconnected (like Lenore and Leo)?

It might be hard to name your feeling other than recognizing that something doesn't feel right—you're experiencing some sort of discomfort. Take the time to reflect and understand your feelings in reaction to others and situations. Recognizing your emotions allows you to understand what drives your reactions and behaviors, including how you communicate. You'll notice emotional patterns by reflecting. Ultimately, reflecting and recognizing your emotional patterns can allow you to pause before reacting impulsively, leading to more measured and intentional responses, improved relationships, and better overall decisions. Self-reflection allows you to learn from experiences, build resilience, and develop emotional intelligence. In the words of Dr. Dan Siegel: "Name it to tame it!"

2. **Ask questions.** Sometimes what we hear is meant exactly as it was communicated, but other times, the messenger may have misspoken or we may have misinterpreted the message. Asking questions is a great way to clarify the message that was intended or reduce potential misunderstandings. Take the first scenario, for example. Instead of remaining silent and having my own thoughts, I could have asked one or a combination of questions:

"Did you just say I will never find work in Boston coming from Midwest regional universities?"

By repeating what I heard, it gives the other person the courtesy of restating and clarifying their comment or confirming it. If that is indeed what was meant to be said and I'm feeling offended, I could have asked follow-up questions, such as:

"Why would you say this? [I'm curious. Do you have direct experience with the universities where I earned my degrees? My experiences there were exceptional.]

"What do you know about my capabilities other than where I went to college?" [I get the sense that you think that I'll be judged by potential employers based on the universities I've attended rather than my skill set and exceptional academic experiences I had there.]

Asking questions requires presence of mind, a calm demeanor, and the courage to engage in potential confrontation. As first-generation professionals, we may feel intimidated by those with more power or prestige and instinctively avoid conflict. But taking the easy way out allows assumptions to linger—sometimes for years, preventing growth and understanding for everyone involved.

3. **Reframe the situation.** There's an ancient Native American expression that a problem is like a pumpkin: you should view the pumpkin from all sides before cutting into it. Reframing an awkward or difficult conversation or situation around class, begins by "walking around the pumpkin." By looking at the situation from different perspectives, you might choose to respond by lifting up your first-gen status—pointing out the unique strengths that come from your lived experience. Alternatively, there might not have been any ill intent, like Scenario 1B, and the conversation doesn't need to be about class. A core underlying issue is determining whether the challenge stems from a blind spot on the part of the speaker or a limited perspective on your own part. In other words, it's important to consider multiple possibilities: The other person may genuinely lack awareness of class dynamics and how they affect interactions. Alternatively, you may be especially attuned to class-related cues due to your own lived experience, which could heighten your sensitivity in ways that others don't immediately understand. It's also possible

that the discomfort has little or nothing to do with class at all and may instead be rooted in different communication styles or other dynamics. Taking the time to reflect on these different dimensions can lead to a more informed interpretation of the situation and open up new, more constructive options for how to engage or move forward.

What if we were more open about our feelings, background and the values we bring to the conversations and relationships? Why not challenge the narratives that make us feel the need to hide?

RESOURCES

We've put together this list of resources that have helped us while working on this guidebook and with first-gen college students and grads. These resources dive deeper into all the topics we cover in *What If...Why Not?* Some of them might even be useful for more than one chapter!

Chapter 1: Before the Job Search

Brooks, K. 2021. *What Color Is Your Parachute? for College: Pave Your Path from Major to Meaningful Work.* Ten Speed Press.

Career and Assessment Tools (free or at a nominal cost)

1. **Career One Stop**: features self-assessment and career exploration tools.

   Website: https://www.careeronestop.org

2. **Strengths Quest**: measures your natural patterns of thinking, feeling, and behaving, and describes your strengths. ($20)

Website: https://www.gallup.com/cliftonstrengths
forstudents

3. **16 Personalities**—starts with Myers-Briggs dichotomies and adds archetypes from Jungian theory as well as some from the Big Five.

Website: https://www.gallup.com/cliftonstrengths
forstudents

4. **VIA Character Strengths Survey**: free, scientific survey to discover character strengths to apply in everyday life.

Website: https://www.viacharacter.org/survey/
account/register

Chapter 2: Landing Your First Job After College

Dalton, S. 2020. *The 2-Hour Job Search: Using Technology to Get the Right Job FASTER*. 2nd ed. Ten Speed Press.

Dalton, S. 2021. *The Job Closer: Time-Saving Techniques for Acing resumes, Interviews, Negotiations, and More*. Ten Speed Press.

Danielle, B. 2024. *The Ultimate Interview Guide: Strategies for Success*. eBook.

Reeves, A. F. 2022. *College to Career Explained: Tools, Skills, and Confidence for Your Job Search*. Agile Consulting Enterprises.

Chapter 3: Common Personal Barriers

Brown, B. 2020. *The Gifts of Imperfection: Let Go of Who You Think You're Supposed to Be and Embrace Who You Are*. Hazelden Publishing.

Nagoski, E., and A. Nagoski. 2019. *Burnout: The Secret to Unlocking the Stress Cycle*. Ballantine Books.

Richo, D. 2021. *How to Be an Adult in Relationships: The Five Keys to Mindful Loving*. Shambhala.

Wiest, B. 2020. *The Mountain Is You: Transforming Self-Sabotage into Self-Mastery*. Thought Catalog Books.

Chapter 4: Utilizing Mentors

Black, Victoria. 2019. "Are You Mentorable." TED Talk. Watch at: https://ideas.ted.com/are-you-mentorable

Chapter 5: Financial Advice

Bernstein, W. J. 2014. *If You Can: How Millennials Can Get Rich Slowly*. Efficient Frontier Publications.

Lindauer, M., T. Larimore, and M. LeBoeuf. 2014. *The Bogleheads' Guide to Investing*. 2nd ed. Wiley.

Wealth Redefined, hosted by Michael Reynolds, CFP. This podcast offers practical insights on money with a modern approach to building wealth and can be heard on Apple Podcasts and Spotify.

Listen at: https://podcasts.apple.com/us/podcast/wealth-redefined/id1462086435 or https://open.spotify.com/show/5TocKyNdsaWiUA1cPOrMPC

The Ramsey Show, hosted by Dave Ramsey and his team, provides straightforward financial advice on paying off debt and building wealth. It can be heard on Apple Podcasts and Spotify or watch full episodes on the Ramsey Show YouTube channel.

Listen at: https://podcasts.apple.com/us/podcast/the-ramsey-show/id77001367 or https://open.spotify.com/show/5exfRPDNCBHmntEkJrILmX

Watch at: https://www.youtube.com/@TheRamseyShow Episodes?app=desktop

Chapter 6: Developing as a Professional

White, T. 2023. *The Unspoken Truths for Career Success: Navigating Pay, Promotions, and Power at Work*. HarperCollins Leadership.

Chapter 7: Navigating and Advancing Your Career

Anderson, C. 2017. *TED Talks: The Official TED Guide to Public Speaking*. Houghton Mifflin Harcourt.

Leaves on a Stream (video on processing emotions). Watch at: https://www.youtube.com/watch?v=vjKltKKSur8

Washington, E. F. 2022. "Recognizing and Responding to Microaggressions at Work." *Harvard Business Review*, May 10.

Chapter 8: Work-Life Balance

A Valuable Lesson for a Happier Life (video). Watch at: https://www.youtube.com/watch?v=SqGRnlXplx0

Ehrnstrom, C., and A. L. Brosse. 2016. *End the Insomnia Struggle: A Step-by-Step Guide to Help You Get to Sleep and Stay Asleep*. New Harbinger Publication.

ABOUT THE AUTHOR

Susan Gershenfeld, PhD, MBA, MSW, has dedicated her career to creating opportunities for others, serving in leadership roles across state government, universities, and professional associations. For over fifteen years, she has championed the success of low-income, first-generation college students—most recently as the founder and CEO of FirstGen Ahead. Her vision for this guidebook is shaped by her own journey as a first-generation college graduate, extensive research, and hands-on work. She is driven by a steadfast belief that talented, hardworking students deserve the chance to thrive and reach their full potential.

ABOUT THE CONTRIBUTORS

Lois A. Benishek, PhD, is a psychologist who has used her degrees in multicultural counseling and counseling psychology in a range of professional positions, that of faculty member, university administrator, addictions researcher, psychotherapist, and career coach. As a first-gen, one of her core missions is to help other first-gens navigate their academic and professional terrains in a way that makes their paths less rocky than hers was. As a lifelong optimist, one of her favorite first-gen mottos is "I never lose. I either win or learn." (Nelson Mandela).

Shanicka S. Burdine, MA, MHRIR, is from Chicago, Illinois. She attended the University of Illinois Urbana-Champaign, earning a bachelor of arts in sociology with a minor in gender and women's studies and a master's in human resources and industrial relations. Also, she holds a master's in organizational leadership with a concentration in higher education and training and development as well as a master's certification in organizational leadership and coaching from Lewis University. She has held various leadership positions at top colleges and universities and multibillion-dollar corporations. Without family and mentorship, she would not be the person she is today. The personal motto she lives by is "it's not enough to be at the table; it's all about what you're doing with your seat there to help others."

Annalea Forrest, MPH, MSW, ACSW, has over ten years of practice in the mental health field, with two master's degrees and two bachelor's degrees focusing on mental health. Annalea is currently a clinical therapist and CEO of Forrest Collective Health LLC, an innovative public health strategy center that focuses on bridging gaps in mental health care in rural and inner-city areas. Annalea's passion for accessible care is driven by her cultural experiences, being a first-generation college student, foster care graduate, and formerly houseless youth.

Janel McNuckle, MHRIR, PHR, SHRM-CP, is a first-generation college graduate and a proud alumna of the University of Illinois at Urbana-Champaign, where she earned both her under-graduate and master's degrees. With over ten years of experience as an HR professional, she has worked across diverse sectors, including nonprofits, sports, and technology. Outside of work, Janel enjoys savoring a perfectly crafted latte, listening to true crime podcasts, and traveling to music festivals across the country. Connect with Janel on LinkedIn: https://www.linkedin.com/in/janelmcnuckle/ or follow her on Instagram: @whatsgoodjoe.

ENDNOTES

[i] This finding is from the Burning Glass Institute and Strada Education Foundation's 2024 report, "Talent Disrupted College Graduates, Underemployment, and the Way Forward," which is an update of their 2018 report, "The Permanent Detour."

[ii] CNBC in 2024 reported some estimates suggest that up to 70 percent of all jobs are not published on publicly available job search sites, and research has long shown that anywhere from half to upward of 80 percent of jobs are filled through networking.

[iii] College graduation rates are different for adults with and without a college-educated parent. The percent of first-gen adults who have at least completed a bachelor's degree is 26 versus 70 percent for continuing gen adults. Source: Pew Research Center analysis of 2019 Survey of Household Economics and Decision-Making.

[iv] This statistic is from the 2024 MentorcliQ Mentoring Impact Report. It's important to note not all mentoring programs are the same, and neither are the outcomes. What's notable is the increase in companies that offer mentoring

programs. Just a few years ago, 70 percent of Fortune 500 companies offered mentoring programs, and this statistic was frequently noted in a variety of publications, including Harvard Business Review and Forbes.

[v] National Association of Colleges and Employers (NACE) conducts the annual "Job Outlook" survey that gathers insights from employers regarding their hiring intentions and the key competencies they value in new college graduates.

[vi] About ten years ago, John Pencavel from Stanford looked into how working hours affect productivity. He found that after working fifty hours a week, output drops fast. After fifty-five hours, it sinks—so much so that working seventy hours doesn't get you anything extra for those extra fifteen hours. More recent research in Iceland on four-day workweeks found that employees felt better—less stress, less burnout, better health, and a better work-life balance.

INDEX